PREDICTING VIOLENT BEHAVIOR

Volume

RECENT VOLUMES IN SAGE LIBRARY OF SOCIAL RESEARCH

95 Roberts **Afro-Arab Fraternity**
96 Rutman **Planning Useful Evaluations**
97 Shimanoff **Communication Rules**
98 Laguerre **Voodoo Heritage**
99 Macarov **Work and Welfare**
100 Bolton **The Pregnant Adolescent**
101 Rothman **Using Research in Organizations**
102 Sellin **The Penalty of Death**
103 Studer/Chubin **The Cancer Mission**
104 Beardsley **Redefining Rigor**
105 Small **Was War Necessary?**
106 Sanders **Rape & Women's Identity**
107 Watkins **The Practice of Urban Economics**
108 Clubb/Flanigan/Zingale **Partisan Realignment**
109 Gittell **Limits to Citizen Participation**
110 Finsterbusch **Understanding Social Impacts**
111 Scanzoni/Szinovacz **Family Decision-Making**
112 Lidz/Walker **Heroin, Deviance and Morality**
113 Shupe/Bromley **The New Vigilantes**
114 Monahan **Predicting Violent Behavior**
115 Britan **Bureaucracy and Innovation**
116 Massarik/Kaback **Genetic Disease Control**
117 Levi **The Coming End of War**
118 Beardsley **Conflicting Ideologies in Political Economy**
119 LaRossa/LaRossa **Transition to Parenthood**
120 Alexandroff **The Logic of Diplomacy**

PREDICTING VIOLENT BEHAVIOR

An Assessment of Clinical Techniques

JOHN MONAHAN

Introduction by **Stanley L. Brodsky**
Foreword by **Saleem A. Shah**

Volume 114
SAGE LIBRARY OF
SOCIAL RESEARCH

SAGE PUBLICATIONS Beverly Hills London

For information address:

SAGE Publications, Inc.
275 South Beverly Drive
Beverly Hills, California 90212

SAGE Publications Ltd
28 Banner Street
London EC1Y 8QE, England

Printed in the United States of America

Library of Congress Cataloging in Publication Data

Monahan, John, 1946-
Predicting violent behavior.

(Sage library of social research ; v. 114)
Bibliography: p.
1. Violence–Prediction. 2. Prediction (Psychology)
3. Psychodiagnostics. I. Title. II. Series.
RC569.5.V55M65 616.85'84 81-851
ISBN 0-8039-1313-3 AACR2
ISBN 0-8039-1314-1 (pbk.)

THIRD PRINTING, 1983

CONTENTS

INTRODUCTION

A haze surrounds this whole topic of violence prediction and dangerousness assessment. It's much like the problem of pollution in our metropolitan city skies; it's damned by everybody, but everybody has to live with it. And so it is with violence prediction: damned by everybody, but our society and legal system surely have to live with it. Indeed, if any changes about violence prediction are occurring in statutory and case law, they are to increase the role of such predictions in custodial decisions about mental patients of criminal offenders. The requirement for involuntary commitment of mental patients, for example, has been redefined by many states using descriptors such as clear, cogent, and compelling evidence of dangerousness, or recent, overt, demonstrated violent behaviors.

This accelerated emphasis on violence potential has been accompanied by a parallel growth in condemnation of violence prediction. On the one hand are the moral condemnations, that it is evil to predict violence, for the poor, the minorities, and the powerless quickly acquire labels as dangerous, and societal patterns of discrimination are extended further on them. On the other hand are the scientific condemnations, which hold that violence does not lend itself to being predicted. The scientific criticisms point out the difficulty of predicting any rare event and call attention to the miserable record of violence predictors in most research studies.

The condemnations don't work, at least in terms of stopping violence prediction. Many clinicians are legally mandated to make such judgments, and psychiatrists, psychologists, and other mental health professionals do continue to predict violence. Without doubt, their attitudes have become questioning, sometimes bitter and cynical. Yet out of occupational requirement or personal belief in what they do, they continue.

In this context, *Predicting Violent Behavior* is an enormously needed contribution. While acknowledging the professional nihilism and the foundations upon which the nihilism was built, Monahan constructs a positive competing frame of reference. What *is* known, and what *can* be predicted, for whom, and when, are his building blocks.

With sensitivity and care, John Monahan examines the ethical dilemmas that swirl around the prediction of violence. No absolute answers are provided, but the issues raised and the struggles with difficult dangerousness-related problems open the way for clinicians in general to follow.

Partial answers are founded in actuarial information. The prediction of violence does have baseline information about incidence and risk. A portion of the answer falls in the extension of clinical findings. Thus, the clinical predictor is advised to consider the cognitive, emotional, and behavioral instigations toward violence, as well as the same sets of factors that inhibit violent behavior. Finding the situational components is advised, so that predictions are not made unequivocally, but rather are reported "given these conditions and circumstances." This trend has existed in psychology for decades, in philosophies ranging from the phenomenological views of Constance Fischer and others in personality assessment, to that of Norman Farberow and his colleagues in suicide prevention. Yet the Monahan book represents the first systematic extrapolation of this clinical perspective into the prediction of violence.

This whole field of violence prediction has been viewed as dirty and vague, and it has not been an enviable task to bring order to it. But Monahan has brought order to it and has accomplished this task with clarity and purpose. With the implemention of these procedures, we may be closer to being in a position to say to the nihilistic critics that they won't have violence prediction to kick around any more.

Stanley L. Brodsky

FOREWORD

The prediction of dangerous and violent behavior is a topic that continues to be the subject of much controversy and discussion in the criminal justice and mental health systems. Decision-makers in both systems are frequently called upon or even required to consider the likelihood that particular individuals will or will not engage in future acts of violence against other persons or against themselves. And, not infrequently, the judgments that are made can have serious consequences for the individuals concerned—and also for segments of the community that might be placed at risk.

In their efforts to reach responsible judgments pertaining to an individual's dangerousness, the criminal and civil justice systems have often sought assistance from mental health professionals. And, while such collaboration between the two systems has had its useful aspects, it has also come under much criticism in recent years. Serious questions have been raised about the absence of sound and empirical evidence that mental health professionals have any special expertise when it comes to making reliable and accurate predictions concerning violent and other dangerous behaviors. It has further been noted, and to some extent demonstrated, that courts and other criminal justice agencies have tended to place rather heavy, and even undue, reliance on the opinions of mental health professionals when reaching decisions that involve not only mental health concerns but also legal, judicial, and public policy considerations.

The difficulties already alluded to could rather easily be resolved if some reliable instruments were readily available for the prediction of violent behaviors. Unfortunately, such instruments do not exist; and it is doubtful that they will ever attain the degree of reliability and accuracy that might be desired. It has been and will remain a very difficult task to predict events that typically have relatively low rates of occurrence within an individual's life time, e.g., serious acts of violence. But, even given this circumstance, there are steps that can be taken to achieve improvements in the quality of the predictive information needed by various decisionmakers.

In this monograph, Dr. John Monahan provides a comprehensive review and discussion of the extant scientific and technical literature pertaining to the prediction of individual violent behavior. The literature is first used to explicate the technical problems associated with such predictions, and then this material is drawn upon as a means of indicating various steps that can be taken to improve the reliability of such predictions and to reduce the error rates.

Dr. Monahan, by training a psychologist, has excellent and impressive credentials as an expert on matters pertaining to the prediction of violence. He has written extensively on this topic in recent years, has served on several task forces and professional committees dealing with this topic, has testified before legislative bodies, and his writings have been cited in several judicial opinions.

This publication is one of several monographs that have been developed by this center during the past 10 years on topics pertaining to interactions between the legal and mental health systems. Previous monographs have included *Competency to Stand Trial and Mental Illness* (1973, reprinted 1977), *Mental Health and Law: A System in Transition* (1975, reprinted 1976), *Criminal Commitments and Dangerous Mental Patients: Legal Issues of Confinement, Treatment and Release* (1976, reprinted 1977), *Dangerous Behavior: A Problem in Law and Mental Health* (1978) and *Legal Aspects of the Enforced Treatment of Offenders* (1979).

It is our hope that, like its predecessors in this series, Dr. Monahan's monograph will be of interest and value to mental health professionals, lawyers, judges, legislators, administrators, and other persons concerned with issues pertaining to the prediction and management of dangerous and violent behavior.

Saleem A. Shah, Ph.D.
Chief, Center for Studies of Crime
and Delinquency

PREFACE

At several points in its gestation, *Predicting Violent Behavior* had a working subtitle. When I was beginning the monograph, it was "Why You Can't Do It." About halfway through writing it, I changed the subtitle to "How to Do It and Why You Shouldn't." By the time I was finished, I was toying with "How to Do It and When to Do It." The development of my thinking on the prediction of violence is reflected quite well in these changes: from an empirical distaste for the task, to an ethical aversion to engaging in it, to a reluctant concession that there may be circumstances in which prediction is both empirically possible and ethically appropriate.

The purpose of this work should thus be clear at the outset. *It is to assist the practicing mental health professional in understanding the issues involved in violence prediction and so to improve the appropriateness and accuracy of his or her clinical predictions.*

Since developed theories and definitive research do not exist merely to be "translated" into clinically relevant terms, I often had to develop theoretical linkages and make empirical assumptions in order to present a framework of any coherence. I learned a great deal in so doing, academic invention once again being parented by clinical necessity. I hope, in other words, that the monograph is of value to researchers and theoreticians in

AUTHOR'S NOTE: This book was prepared under a contract from the Center for Studies of Crime and Delinquency, National Institute of Mental Health.

the area and to those in the criminal justice system who deal with violent behavior.

Work on this monograph began while I was a Fellow in Law and Psychology at Harvard Law School, and my thinking on prediction evolved substantially through my contact there with Alan Dershowitz and Alan Stone. It continued at the law school of the University of California, Los Angeles, where Deans Warren and Bauman graciously provided me with an office. The monograph was completed while I was a visiting scholar at Stanford Law School, a position generously arranged by David Rosenhan.

Several persons reviewed and commented upon early drafts of this monograph, and I am grateful for their time and insight: Loren Roth, Raymond Novaco, Leah McDonough, Michael Widdon, and Mary Ruggiero. Stanley Brodsky and several of his students were especially helpful in their suggestions for improvement.

Saleem Shah provided a meticulous and pentrating analysis of an earlier version of this work that greatly improved the final product.

Paul Meehl provided very valuable advice on several key issues in prediction, although he may wish that I took more of it.

While it would please me greatly to share with these colleagues responsibility for any errors and omissions in the monograph along with their deserved kudos for what others may find useful, an unfortunate tradition not of my making insists that I hold them blameless.

John Monahan
Charlottesville, Virginia

Chapter 1

INTRODUCTION TO A CONTROVERSY

PREDICTION IN LIFE AND IN LAW

Predicting who among us will commit a violent act has been called "the paramount consideration in the law-mental health system" by the President of the American Psychiatric Association (Stone 1975) and "the greatest unresolved problem the criminal justice system faces" by the President of the National Council on Crime and Delinquency (Rector 1973).

Despite its emergence only recently as the overarching concern in both the mental health and criminal justice systems, predicting harmful conduct in order to take preventive action has existed as long as law itself. Reviewing the history of prediction in Anglo-American law, Dershowitz (1974, p. 57) concluded that "the preventive confinement of dangerous persons who cannot be convicted of past criminality but who are thought likely to cause serious injury in the future has always been practiced, to some degree, by every society in history regardless of the jurisprudential rhetoric employed." "Moreover," he noted, "it is likely that some forms of preventive confinement will continue to be practiced by every society."

Far from being the occult crystal-ball activity it sometimes is made to appear, prediction is part of life. The human race would not have survived as long as it has were our ancestors not adept at predicting in some rough and intuitive way what nature had in store for them, such as that lions may bite and falling rocks crush, so it is best to avoid both whenever possible. Predictions of the movement of the stars and the rising of the tides were among the first scientific puzzles to preoccupy humankind. On a more contemporary level, much of our own lives is spent predicting how others will respond to us, and we to them, as lover, friend, or colleague. The prediction of harm is likewise pervasive: We drive through green lights only because we predict that cross-traffic will stop on the red.

The mental health and criminal justice systems, as codifications of socially acceptable human interaction, rely heavily upon predictive decisionmaking. Shah (1978a, p. 225) has recently enumerated the points in the legal process at which estimates of future harmful conduct are taken (see also Rennie 1978):

1. Decisions concerning bail, or release on personal recognizance for persons accused of crimes, including the level at which the bail is to be set
2. Decisions concerning the waiver to adult courts of juveniles charged with serious crimes
3. Sentencing decisions following criminal convictions, including decisions about release on conditions of probation
4. Decisions pertaining to work-release and furlough programs for incarcerated offenders
5. Parole and other conditional release decisions for offenders
6. Decisions pertaining to the commitment and release of "sexual psychopaths," "sexually dangerous persons," "defective delinquents," and the like
7. Determinations of dangerousness for all indicted felony defendants found incompetent to stand trial (e.g., in New York State)[1]
8. Decisions pertaining to the special handling of and transfer to special prisons of offenders who are disruptive in regular prisons
9. Commitment of drug addicts (because of fears that they will commit violent crimes to support their drug habit)
10. Decisions concerning the emergency and longer term involuntary commitment of mentally ill persons considered to pose a "danger to self or others"

11. Decisions concerning the "conditional" and "unconditional" release of involuntarily confined mental patients
12. Decisions concerning the hospitalization (on grounds of continuing mental disorder and dangerousness) of persons acquitted by reason of insanity
13. Decisions regarding the transfer to security hospitals of mental patients found to be too difficult or dangerous to be handled in regular civil mental hospitals
14. Decisions concerning the invocation of special legal proceedings or sentencing provision for "habitual" and "dangerous" offenders
15. Decisions concerning the likelihood of continued dangerousness of persons convicted of capital crimes, as a basis for determination regarding the use of the death sentence

Regarding this last point, the U.S. Supreme Court held that it was not unconstitutional for a State to make the imposition of the death penalty on an offender convicted of certain categories of murder contingent upon a prediction that he or she would be violent in the future. "It is, of course, not easy to predict future behavior. The fact that such a determination is difficult, however, does not mean that it cannot be made" (*Jurek v. Texas* 1976).

For a variety of reasons, to be discussed below, the legal system typically relies upon psychiatrists and psychologists to provide estimates of the potential for future harm, although computer-generated tables are sometimes used in the case of parole.

Before discussing how predictions of harmful conduct can best be made, it is necessary to consider what it is that is being predicted and whether one should be engaged in predicting it at all.

DEFINITIONS OF DANGEROUS AND VIOLENT BEHAVIOR

At first glance, the definition of "violent" or "dangerous" behavior appears to be a straightforward one about which only academics could quibble. Being shot, stabbed, or punched is violent. The meaning of a sign reading "dangerous" placed behind a gasoline truck or near a patch of thin ice is likewise clear. Yet as soon as one goes beyond these obvious examples, problems arise (Brooks 1978). While Sarbin (1967) cogently distinguishes between violence and dangerousness ("Violence denotes action; danger denotes a relationship"), virtually all others hold the terms synonymous. Some define violence to include only injury or death to *persons* (e.g., Rubin 1972), while others include the destruction of *property* (e.g., Mulvihill and Tumin 1969). Violent thoughts are considered dangerous by some "because patients with fears and fantasies of violence sometimes act them out" (Ervin and Lion 1969). A Federal court once ruled that writing a bad check was a sufficiently "dangerous" behavior to justify commitment (*Overholser v. Russell* 1960), since the economy would collapse if everyone did it.

The Model Sentencing Act defined two types of dangerous offenders: "(1) the offender who has committed a serious crime against a person and shows a behavior pattern of persistent assaultiveness based on serious mental disturbance and (2) the offender deeply involved in organized crime" (National Council on Crime and Delinquency, 1973, p. 456). The act commented that in no State would such offenders total more than 100 at any given time. One may wonder, however, about the harmlessness of an offender who has committed a serious crime against a person and shows a behavior pattern of persistent assaultiveness *without* having a serious mental disturbance. Note that if one considers all repetitive violent offenders to have a serious mental disturbance one has reduced the concept of mental disturbance to a tautology.

The working definition of violence adopted by the National Commission on the Causes and Prevention of Violence (Mulvihill and Tumin 1969) was "overtly threatened or overtly accomplished application of force which results in the injury or destruction of persons or property or reputation, or the illegal appropriation of property." Megargee (1969) notes that such a definition would include as violent: accidental homicide, homicide in self-defense, or injury on the football field. He states that two issues confound the framing of a completely acceptable definition of violence. The first of these is legality. By ignoring legality and focusing on the act itself, the Commission has unwittingly characterized as violent various legal injuries to people. The alternative of defining violence in terms of illegal acts, however, "is to classify as nonviolent the behavior of Nazi genocidists or Roman gladiators . . ." (p. 1039). The second nemesis of obtaining an acceptable definition of violence is the question of intentionality. The Commission's definition includes unintentional or accidental violence. The alternative of specifying that violence can only be intentional or conscious would not hold well with those of psychoanalytic bent.

This confusion in the specification of "dangerous" acts has been noted by the U.S. Court of Appeals (D.C. Circuit) in *Cross* v. *Harris* (1969), a case which held that "a finding of 'dangerousness' must be based on a high probability of substantial injury." The court stated that some framework is needed to specify which acts are dangerous and which are not.

> Without some such framework, "dangerous" could readily become a term of art describing anyone whom we would, all things considered, prefer not to encounter on the streets. We did not suppose that Congress had used "dangerous" in any such Pickwickian sense. Rather, we supposed that Congress intended the courts to refine the unavoidably vague concept of "dangerousness" on a case-by-case basis, in the traditional common-law fashion (p. 1099).

It may be best, however, to avoid terms that are "unavoidably vague." "Dangerousness" confuses issues regarding *what* one is predicting with the *probability* one is assigning to its prediction. The word has a tendency in practice to degenerate from a characteristic of behavior to a reified personality trait. "Hence, through a conceptual shortcut, first certain aspects of an individual's *behavior* are defined as dangerous, and the *individual himself* comes to be viewed and labeled as dangerous" (Shah 1977, p. 105).

The "prediction of dangerous behavior" is even more troublesome. "Dangerous behavior" may be thought of as a prediction in itself. It is a *conditional* probability. *If* one steps on dangerously thin ice, *then* one will fall in the water. If not, one is safe. *If* one corners a dangerous turn too fast, *then* one will drive off the road. If not, one will drive on (cf. Gordon 1977).

It may be conceptually crisper to refer only to "violent behavior" (or "violence"). These terms may simplify the separation of definitional issues from probabilistic ones and keep the focus on actions rather than on personalities. As Scott (1977, p. 128) concluded, "the available definitions of 'dangerousness' may be thought to be so unsatisfactory that it would be better for most purposes to substitute a probability figure of this or that sort of damaging behavior occurring in this or that expected environment." In this monograph, violent behavior will be defined as Megargee (1976, p. 12) has defined it: "*acts characterized by the application or overt threat of force which is likely to result in injury to people.*" "Injury" shall be taken to mean "physical injury." The notion of "threat" is included so that the definition will encompass armed robbery or other situations in which injury is threatened but not accomplished. The notion of "likely" is included so that shooting at someone will be considered violent even if the bullets miss. As Megargee (1976, p. 5) states:

> This use of the term includes, but is not restricted to, such criminal acts as homicide, mayhem, aggravated assault, forcible rape, battery, robbery, arson, and extortion. Criminal behaviors not likely to result in injury to people, such as noncoercive thefts or vandalism, are excluded, as are business practices which, although injurious to people, do not involve the application of force.

It is important to distinguish between the *description* and the *evaluation* of violent acts. Because a given act is judged to be "legal" or "legitimate," e.g., a citizen killing in self-defense, a police officer shooting a fleeing felon, does not make it any less violent for descriptive purposes.

CRITICISMS OF PREDICTION IN LAW

Prediction, we have noted, has always been a part of life and has always been a part of law. Yet one would have to be completely out of touch with recent developments in criminal and mental health law not to notice that the prediction of violent behavior by mental health professionals has been under sustained attack. These criticisms and the issues they raise are examined so that the reader may put the remaining chapters into perspective.

The three criticisms are (1) that it is empirically impossible to predict violent behavior; (2) that, even if such activity could be forecast and averted, it would, as a matter of policy, violate the civil liberties of those being predicted; and (3) that even if accurate prediction were possible without violating civil liberties, psychiatrists and psychologists should decline to do it, since it is a social control activity at variance with their professional helping role.

THE EMPIRICAL ATTACK: ACCURATE PREDICTION IS IMPOSSIBLE

Rarely have research data been as quickly or nearly universally accepted by the academic and professional communities as those supporting the proposition that mental health professionals are highly inaccurate at predicting violent behavior. We shall consider prediction research in detail in subsequent chapters, but the reader had best be forewarned that stock in the predictive enterprise is going very cheaply.

A task force of the American Psychiatric Association concluded that "the state of the art regarding predictions of violence is very unsatisfactory. The ability of psychiatrists or any other professionals to reliably predict future violence is unproved" (1974, p. 30).

In 1978, a task force of the American Psychological Association reached a similar conclusion:

> It does appear from reading the research that the validity of psychological predictions of dangerous behavior, at least in the sentencing and release situation we are considering, is extremely poor, so poor that one could oppose their use on the strictly empirical grounds that psychologists are not professionally competent to make such judgments (p. 1110).

With few exceptions, individual psychiatrists and psychologists prominent in the area have echoed their association's warnings. Halleck (1967), for example, noted that "if the psychiatrist or any other behavioral scientist were asked to show proof of his predictive skills, objective data could not be offered" (p. 314). Diamond (1974, p. 452) has written:

> Neither psychiatrists nor other behavioral scientists are able to predict the occurrence of violent behavior with sufficient reliability to justify the restriction of freedom of persons on the basis of the label of potential dangerousness. Accordingly, it is recommended that courts no longer ask such experts to give their opinion of the potential dangerousness of any person, and that psychiatrists and other behavioral scientists acknowledge their inability to make such prediction when called upon to do so by courts and other legal agencies.

Attorneys in the mental health area have shared these conclusions. Dershowitz concluded that "for every correct psychiatric prediction of violence, there are numerous erroneous predictions" (1969, p. 47). The latest edition of the American Civil Liberties Union Handbook, *The Rights of Mental Patients* (Ennis and Emery 1978), states that "it now seems beyond dispute that mental health professionals have *no* expertise in predicting future dangerous behavior either to self or others. In fact, predictions of dangerous behavior are wrong about 95 percent of the time" (p. 20; italics in original).

Kahle and Sales (1980) surveyed several hundred practicing psychiatrists, clinical psychologists, and mental health lawyers in a national study of attitudes toward civil commitment. They asked the respondents to estimate the "percentage of accurate predictions which are made with current methods of predicting dangerousness to others." The groups did not differ significantly among themselves. The mean estimates of predictive accuracy were between 40 and 46 percent.

THE POLITICAL ATTACK: PREDICTION VIOLATES CIVIL LIBERTIES

Originally voiced by Szasz, the position that preventive or therapeutic intervention based upon a prediction of future behavior violates the most fundamental rights guaranteed in a democratic society–punishment for past acts, not detention for future acts–has gained a large number of adherents. As Szasz (1963) originally put it:

> The ghost of the "dangerous mental patient" will not be laid to rest until it is recognized that the institution to which the so-called mental patient is committed is not a hospital but a prison. Lawbreakers, irrespective of their mental health, ought to be treated as offenders. This would afford possibilities for "therapy" in a context in which personal liberties could be protected; whereas our present practices, which use civil law to deprive people of their liberties, make both therapy and the protection of civil rights impossible (pp. 144-5).

Indeed, the very designation of an act as "dangerous" or "violent" reflects political values that some may find unacceptable.

> Drunken drivers are dangerous both to themselves and to others. They injure and kill many more people than, for ample, persons with paranoid delusions of persecution. Yet, people labeled "paranoid" are readily committable, while drunken drivers are not.
>
> Some types of dangerous behavior are even rewarded. Racecar drivers, trapeze artists, and astronaughts receive admiration and applause. In contrast, the poly-surgical addict and the would-be suicide receive nothing but contempt and aggression. Indeed, the latter type of dangerousness is considered a good cause for commitment. Thus, it is not dangerousness in general that is at issue here, but rather the manner in which one is dangerous (Szasz 1963, p. 46).

The most recent frontal political assault on the use of predictions of violent behavior has occurred in the context of criminal sentencing. The "just deserts" model of imprisonment, which has been adopted by many States, explicitly eschews reliance upon predictive considerations in determining an offender's release from prison (von Hirsch 1976; Twentieth Century Fund 1976). In its place is an explicitly normative and moral judgment of relative harm and the offender's culpability for having committed it.

> [P]redictive restraint poses special ethical problems. The fact that the person's liberty is at stake reduces the moral acceptability of mistakes of overprediction. Moreover, one may question whether it is ever just to *punish* someone more severely for what he is expected to do, even if the prediction was accurate (von Hirsch 1976, p. 26; italics in original).

THE PROFESSIONAL ATTACK: PREDICTION DESTROYS THE HELPING ROLE OF THE MENTAL HEALTH DISCIPLINES

After years of being blasted as empirically incompetent to predict violent behavior and crypto-fascists if they even tried, some mental health professionals have made a counterattack. They not only have outflanked their critics by *agreeing* that accurate prediction is factually impossible and politically improper, but have gone them one better by asserting that the prediction of violence and subsequent interventions to avert it are not—and, in fact, never were—within the purview of the mental health professions. It was the legal system that asked the psychiatrist and psychologist to give opinions regarding violence potential for use in civil commitment and other proceedings. If mental health professionals naively acquiesced, they have now discovered that this incursion into forecasting the future was a mistake. It was a mistake not simply because research allegedly showed the effort to be fruitless or because political rights were trampled, but because in the process the mental health professional gave up his or her essential role as a healer of psychic pain and became an agent of social control. Engaging in the prediction of violence to others "tends to relegate psychiatry to the very role for which it has been criticized, that of valuing societal rights above those of the individual," whereas "our sole aim should be to ensure the welfare of our patients." Thus "the prediction of danger is not within medical competence and under no circumstances should be" (Peszke 1975, pp. 826, 828).

The professional attack on prediction was led by Stone, a psychiatrist on the faculties of the Harvard Law and Medical Schools. Stone, in his highly influential NIMH monograph,

Mental Health and the Law: A System in Transition (1975), proposed a new medical model of civil commitment, openly based on paternalistic concern for the patient's welfare rather than society's protection. His "Thank-you Theory" "divests civil commitment of a police function; dangerous behavior is returned to the province of the criminal law. Only someone who is irrational, treatable, and incidently dangerous would be confined to the mental health system" (p. 70).

Even if accurate prediction could be accomplished with civil liberties safeguarded, many mental health professionals would still be opposed to participating in any scheme that would make them agents of social control rather than benefactors of the welfare of the individual client.

THE MORAL AND POLITICAL ISSUES RAISED BY PREDICTION

The criticisms that have been raised against the use of predictions of violence in criminal and mental health law tend to confound empirical issues with moral and political ones. Even the criticism that violence cannot be predicted accurately enough for use in legal decisionmaking involves a moral and political judgment on the meaning of "enough." It may be beneficial, if only to facilitate rational discourse on the topic, to separate empirical and moral-political questions so that each may receive our undivided attention. Since the empirical issues are considered in later chapters, the moral and political ones are outlined here (cf. Monahan 1980). The four questions of moral and political value inhering in the prediction of violence appear to concern: (a) the nature of what we are predicting; (b) the factors we use to predict it; (c) the degree of predictability that triggers preventive action; and (d) the nature of the preventive action taken.

THE CRITERION: WHY SOME FORMS OF VIOLENCE AND NOT OTHERS?

Szasz' (1963) position on the singling out of the mentally ill for preventive confinement based on a prediction of harm has already been noted. The vagaries of how harm is defined do indeed appear to be substantial. Monahan and Hood (1978) surveyed jurors to find how "dangerous" they perceived a list of behaviors commonly referred to as such in legal and mental health literature. They found that older persons ranked more behaviors as "dangerous" than did younger persons, females more than males, the less educated more than the more educated, and conservatives more than liberals.

Much of the variation in how a harm comes to be officially perceived and designated as a matter of public concern appears to be produced by social and political factors. Monahan, Novaco, and Geis (1979) defined "corporate violence" as "illegal behavior producing an unreasonable risk of physical harm to consumers, employees, or other persons as a result of deliberate decisionmaking by corporate executives or culpable negligence on their part" (cf. Megargee 1976), argued that it is responsible for more deaths and injuries than the more mundane forms of crime, and suggested that the preoccupation of the law and the behavioral sciences with "street" rather than "suite" violence reflects, in part, political and economic biases operating in American society (see also Geis and Monahan 1976; Monahan and Novaco 1980). The very choice of our subject matter, therefore, is a decision laden with moral and political implications.

THE PREDICTORS: WHAT SHALL BE INCLUDED?

As we shall later see, among the principal statistical correlates of future violent behavior are past violence, sex, age, race, socioeconomic status, and heroin or alcohol abuse. *Not* to take these factors into consideration in making predictions is to doom the effort from the start. Yet, many are unwilling to include information that will work to the further disadvantage of precisely those they view as most "victimized" in the past by social injustice (Ryan 1971). As Wilson notes with regard to criminal sentencing, "the things that might be taken into account that are most determinative of criminality—the age, sex, and race of the offender—are precisely those factors that society for perfectly commendable reasons, often wishes not to take into account" (1977, p. 115).

Even the use of prior violent behavior as a predictor of future violence raises moral dilemmas. "If an ex-convict has truly 'paid for his crime,' as is so often said, upon his release from custody or supervision, then it would arguably be morally invalid to exact any further payment from him in later years by giving him a greater sentence than a first offender otherwise similarly situated" (Wilkins et al. 1978, p. 9).

In fact, according to one point of view, racial and economic discrimination, the "diseases" of alcoholism and heroin addiction, and the "macho" demand characteristics of lower class male subculture can be seen as restricting a person's behavioral options and thereby *reducing* the moral acceptability of preventive confinement. Clarence Darrow put this position well in a speech to the prisoners of the Cook County Jail in Chicago in 1902 (quoted in Weinberg 1957, p. 8):

> Long ago, Mr. Buckle, who was a great philosopher and historian, collected facts, and he showed that the number of people who were arrested increased just as the price of food increased. When they put up the price of gas ten cents a thousand, I do not know who will go to jail, but I do know that a certain number of people will go. When the meat combine raises the price of beef, I do not know who is going to go to jail, but I know that a large number of people are bound to go. Whenever the Standard Oil Company raises the price of oil, I know that a certain number of girls who are seamstresses, and who work night after night long hours for somebody else, will be compelled to go out on the streets and ply another trade, and I know that Mr. Rockefeller and his associates are responsible and not the poor girls in the jails.

Apropos of Darrow, Brenner (1977) has recently reported that a 1 percent increase in the national unemployment rate generates a 4 percent increase in the incidence of homicide and a 6 percent increase in the incidence of robbery.

Ideally, one would hope to develop predictors "which would be based only upon statistically valid factors and weights which were simultaneously proper from an ethical standpoint" (Wilkins et al. 1978, p. 8). Yet what does one do when science and morality are at crosspurposes? And how does one take into account "justice" to the potential *victims* of violent crime "who, like their offenders and unlike the legislators, judges, and psychologists making decisions in the criminal justice system, are often poor and nonwhite" (American Psychological Association 1978)?

THE RELATIONSHIP: HOW ACCURATE IS ACCURATE ENOUGH?

All a person predicting violence can hope to do is assign a probability figure to the occurrence of violent behavior by a given individual during a given time period. The figure may be expressed in either arithmetic (e.g., 75 percent likely) or in prose form (e.g., "substantially likely," "more likely than not"). In either case, the question remains, "Is this degree of relationship sufficiently great to justify preventive intervention?", whether that intervention is in the form of civil commitment, denial of parole release, or informing a potential victim. "What represents an acceptable trade-off between the values of public safety and individual liberty?" (Wenk, Robison, and Smith 1972, p. 402). (The answer to the trade-off question may be very different, depending upon the intervention to be taken [see below]). No one insists that prediction be perfect. We do not, after all, require absolute certainty for convicting the guilty, only proof beyond a "reasonable doubt." This means that we are willing to tolerate the conviction of a few innocent persons to assure the confinement of a much larger number of guilty criminals. It also means that, when there is a doubt, we would much rather release a guilty person than confine an innocent one.

But how many persons are we willing to hospitalize, or deep imprisoned, to keep the streets safe from one "dangerous" person? According to Dershowitz (1974, p. 60), "we have not even begun to ask these kinds of questions, or to develop modes of analysis for answering them."

THE CONSEQUENCES: PREDICTION FOR WHAT PURPOSE?

As Shah (1978a) has noted, the consequences accruing to a positive prediction of violent behavior range from denying a work-release program to an incarcerated offender to imposing the death penalty on him or her. Clearly, the moral issues raised by prediction may vary as a function of the uses to which the predictions are put. If one believes that imposing the death penalty is an intrinsically immoral end, then a prediction of violent behavior, as the means to achieving that end, is likewise tainted (see Dix 1977*a*; 1977*b*). It is not surprising that Szasz (1963), who believes civil commitment to be unethical, also abjures the predictions of harm upon which it is often based.

Most would agree that where the "cost" of predicting too many people to have a condition is negligible, and the "benefit" of correctly predicting the true cases is great, prediction is morally acceptable even when extremely inaccurate. Thus, physicians place drops of silver nitrate in the eyes of all newborn infants to prevent blindness resulting from congenital gonorrhea, even though the incidence of congenital gonorrhea is infinitesimal. The erroneously "predicted" babies are not injured, and a great gain–sight–is achieved for the correct predictions (Heller and Monahan 1977).

As the consequences of prediction vary, so may its moral component. In the case of civil commitment, for example, the consequences of long-term hospitalization to the person committed on the basis of an inaccurate prediction of violence are very great. Yet, the situation may be otherwise with predictions of imminent violence which result in "only" several days commitment, after which the person is released. While such detention is plainly a deprivation of liberty, it would be highly disingenuous to compare it to the lifelong confinement so effectively castigated by Szasz (1963) and others. There is, as we shall see, reason to believe that short-term predictions may be more accurate than long-term ones.

Yet with the costs of each so vastly different, it may be possible ethically to justify short-term commitment even if the predictions of

> imminent violence on which it is based are *less* accurate than the long-term research indicates. Paraphrasing Blackstone, it may be better that ten "false positives" suffer commitment *for three days* than that one "false negative" go free to kill someone during that period (Monahan 1977*a*, p. 370).

In this regard, it is sometimes noted that the ability of psychologists and psychiatrists to predict violent behavior is not appreciably worse than their ability to predict job performance, school performance, or many other facets of human behavior (Mischel 1968). The question is whether this observation should make us feel more sanguine about violence prediction or more guarded about prediction in other areas. It may be that the prediction of violence for the purpose of hospitalization or imprisonment is, at its best, no less accurate than the predictions of academic success upon which we base admission to universities and graduate schools, or the predictions of job performance which figure into the hiring of employees for government, industry, and the military. Should this be true, however, it would still not attenuate the urgency of coming to terms with the ethical quandaries of predicting violent behavior. The consequences of erroneous prediction in other areas of life, e.g., a career opportunity closed because one failed to score sufficiently high on a test that had low validity to begin with, may indeed be severe. Yet, the consequences of erroneous predictions of violence include the injury or death of the victim of the person wrongly predicted to be safe and the extended institutionalization in a prison or mental hospital of the person wrongly predicted to be violent, or even, as we have noted, his or her execution. While the prediction of violent behavior shares many features with the prediction of other forms of human conduct, the potential consequences of its misapplication give it a priority in professional and ethical concern.

A STATEMENT OF PERSONAL VALUES

It is clear that the participation of mental health professionals in decisions calling for a prediction of violent behavior is a matter of considerable empirical, political, professional, and moral controversy on which people of equal intelligence and integrity will differ. Since the manner in which one evaluates the evidence on prediction, and even the factors one will admit into evidence (Kuhn 1962) are strongly influenced by one's personal value positions on the questions raised, it may be appropriate to briefly but explicitly state my own current position. In this manner, the reader will be better able to evaluate potential biases in the material that follows. I would stress the word "current," since my own views have evolved substantially in this area and will no doubt continue to do so at a sometimes troubling rate.

Empirically, it is much less clear to me now than it once was that relatively accurate prediction is impossible under all circumstances. As will be discussed, most existing research in this area leaves something to be desired and while much could be done to improve it (Monahan 1978*a*), the practical difficulty of discovering violence when it occurs and the ethical questions involved in doing randomized experiments with possibly violent persons make it doubtful whether definitive tests of predictive accuracy in many situations will *ever* be done (Dox 1976; Monahan 1977*a*).

Further, there are theoretical reasons why *short-term* predictions of violent behavior may be more accurate than the long-term predictions studied to date, and there is a growing body of empirical evidence suggesting that, for the small group of *habitually violent persons,* the probability of future violence is raised considerably.

Rather than *we know it is impossible to accurately predict violent behavior under any circumstances,* I believe a more judicious assessment of the research to date is that *we know very little about how accurately violent behavior may be predicted under many circumstances.*

Politically, I have a great deal of sympathy with the libertarian critics of "preventive justice" (Dershowitz 1973). One cannot read accounts of the horrendous abuses of mental health and penological discretion without being profoundly moved. As a matter of policy, for example, I see little value in psychiatrists and psychologists offering individual clinical predictions of violence for use in setting prison sentences for mentally competent offenders (cf. Monahan and Ruggiero 1980). Here, I am more concerned with justice and deterrence than with predictive accuracy and would limit predictive considerations to a decidedly secondary role.

Yet, even in criminal sentencing, the issue of prediction is politically complex. As the American Psychological Association Task Force on the Role of Psychology in the Criminal Justice System recently stated:

> In those situations where the realistic alternative to distinguishing among offenders on predictive grounds is that a Draconian sentence is uniformly given to all offenders, it is not clear to us that offering such predictions is, on balance, always ethically inappropriate. Nor is there agreement on whether predictive considerations should play a role in decisions regarding the release of certain classes of offenders (e.g., offenders with psychological disorders) from prison to community treatment to serve the length of their sentence (1978, p. 1110).

Professionally, I believe that it would indeed be nice if mental health personnel could leave their current "police power" roles (i.e., their roles as protectors of community safety rather than of the individual client) to those who were sworn police officers and could focus exclusively on promoting their clients' welfare. But it is not clear to me that this is either possible or desirable. Do not all "human service" professions have a social protection component to them? Teachers, for example, whose role is to improve the welfare of their students, surely view themselves primarily as transmitters of knowledge and culture. Yet they frequently function as disciplinarians whose tasks include expelling those whose conduct is detrimental to the learning of others and acting as society's gatekeepers by withholding diplomas needed for jobs and further education from those who do not meet socially defined standards of academic performance. It is as the agents of society, not for the welfare of the individual pupil, that teachers perform these functions.

Likewise and more to the point, nonpsychiatric physicians perform a variety of social control functions with little adverse effect on their primary help-giving role. They can initiate the involuntary detention of persons who through no fault of their own carry contagious diseases. They are bound in many States to report to the police whenever they suspect child abuse to have occurred.

While one would hope that the community protection role of mental health professionals would be minimal relative to their helping functions (as it is with teachers and physicians), it does not seem to me to be unreasonable of society to demand that a limited "police power" function remain (cf. Roth 1979).

In a far-reaching and bitterly contested decision, the California Supreme Court ruled that psychiatrists and psychologists may be liable for civil damages if they fail to inform the prospective victim of a patient they have predicted–or *should* have predicted–to be violent. The court, in other words, imposed a police-power role upon psychotherapists in regard to patients they perceive as violent.

> . . . public policy favoring protection of the confidential character of patient-psychotherapeutic communication must yield in instances in which disclosure is essential to avert danger to others. The protective privilege ends where the public peril begins. (*Tarasoff* v. *Regents of the University of California* 1976, p. 14).

Some mental health professionals see such decisions as driving a stake into the heart of their helping role. I would agree with Shah (1977), however, that this need not be so.

> Some clinicians are utterly convinced that therapeutic confidentiality must remain an *absolute* and paramount value over all other societal interests. Such ethnocentric zeal seems to demand that the entire society should accept the value and ideologies of psychotherapists. In other words, what is good for psychotherapists is good for society! (p. 2, italics in original).

The moral issues raised by prediction are very troubling. At least one would hope that they would trouble both the utilitarians who are tempted to run roughshod over considerations of moral justice and the libertarians who must consider justice to the victims as well as the perpetrators of violent acts. While I am not prepared to offer a prescription for analyzing, much less resolving, the moral quandaries surrounding the predictive enterprise, I do have several biases concerning prerequisites for such analysis and resolution. The first prerequisite is the injection of a large dose of candor into predictive decisionmaking. *The principal impediment to progress in the area of prediction is that most of the difficult problems hide behind a screen of "professional judgment."*

What are we trying to predict? Assault? Property damage? No. We predict "dangerousness."

What factors do we use in making the prediction? Race? Socioeconomic status? No. We rely on "clinical experience."

How likely must a "dangerous" act be to justify intervention? Ninety percent probable? More likely than not? No. We intervene whenever there is a "risk" of harm.

What is to be done on the basis of the prediction? Seventy-two-hour commitment? The death penalty? Far too often, we treat predictions as if they were cheap socks: "One size fits all."

What is necessary for moral and legal (and, as we shall discuss, empirical) progress in the area of prediction is a dramatic increase in the degree to which mental health professionals articulate what it is they are predicting and how they went about predicting it. This involves explicitly enumerating the kinds of acts one takes to be violent, frankly stating the factors on which the prediction is based, and being clear on the likelihood with which it is believed they will occur. One's judgment on all these factors may vary with the purpose to which the prediction is put.

Without such an influx of candor, prediction will rightly continue to be criticized as the imposition of the mental health professionals' personal values on decisions that should be left to others in a democratic society (Morse 1978).

Regardless of whether one is intellectually persuaded to increased explicitness in formulating predictions, courts are beginning to demand as much from the mental health professions. In *Millard* v. *Harris* (1968), the United States Court of Appeals for the District of Columbia stated:

> Predictions of dangerousness . . . require determinations of several sorts: the type of conduct in which the individual may engage; the likelihood or probability that he will in fact engage in that conduct; and the effect such conduct if engaged in will have on others. Depending on the sort of conduct and effect feared, these variables may also require further refinement (p. 973).

In another case, *Cross* v. *Harris,* (1969) the court continued this analysis:

> [It is] particularly important that courts not allow this second question [of likelihood of harm] to devolve by default upon the expert witness. Psychiatrists should not be asked to testify, without more, simply whether future behavior or threatened harm is "likely" to occur. For the psychiatrist "may in his own mind" be defining "likely" to mean anything from virtual certainty to slightly above chance. And his definition will not be a reflection of any expertise, but . . . of his own personal perference for safety or liberty (pp. 1100-1101).

It should be noted that mental health professionals have not so much sought ambiguity in the law regarding prediction in order to enhance their own power as they have had it foisted upon them by legislatures and courts unwilling to face up to difficult moral and policy choices. Why should courts worry about whether the Constitution permits sex or age to be used in an actuarial prediction table for parole release when they can just get a psychiatrist or psychologist to "launder" both these factors into a prediction based on "clinical expertise?" Why should legislators engage in heated debates about the trade-offs between liberty and safety involved in deciding the degree of likelihood of harm that is sufficient to trigger State intervention, when a mental health professional is willing to make the decision for them?

The strategy adopted here is to provide as much information to the legal system as possible regarding the prediction of violent behavior, and then, within some broad moral constraints, to stand back and let the legal system do with it as it will. As one recent report on this topic stated, "Since it is not within the professional competence of psychologists [or psychiatrists] to offer conclusions on matters of law, psychologists [and psychiatrists] should resist pressure to offer such conclusions" (American Psychological Association 1978, p. 1105).

Monahan and Wexler (1978, p. 38), in this regard, argue that when a mental health professional predicts that a person will be "dangerous to others" for the purpose of civil commitment, he or she is making three separable assertions:

1. The individual being examined has certain characteristics.
2. These characteristics are associated with a certain probability of violent behavior.
3. The probability of violent behavior is "sufficiently" great to justify preventive intervention.

The first two of these assertions, Monahan and Wexler hold, are professional judgments within the expertise of the mental health professional (judgments which can, of course, be challenged in court). The third is a social policy statement that must be arrived at through the political process and upon which the mental health professional should have no more say than any other citizen (Morse 1978). What the mental health professional should do, they argue, is present and defend an estimate of the probability that the individual will engage in violent behavior and *leave to judges and legislators—who are the appropriate persons in a democratic society to weigh competing claims among social values—the decision as to whether this probability of violent behavior is sufficient to justify preventive interventions.*

In no sense, for example, do the data on the prediction of violent behavior compel their own policy implications. Given that the level of predictive validity revealed in the research has, in an absolute sense, been rather modest, one could use the data to argue for across-the-board reductions in the length of institutionalization of prisoners and mental patients: Since we cannot be sure who will do us harm, we should detain no one. Alternatively, and with equal fervor and logic, one could use the same data to argue for across-the-board *increases* in the length of institutionalization: Since we cannot be sure which ones will be safe, we should keep them all in. Whether one uses the data in support of one rather than the other of these implications will depend upon how one assesses and weighs the various "costs" and "benefits" associated with each, or upon the nonutilitarian principles for allocating confinement that one adopts (e.g., Rawls 1972; Scharf in press). In regard to the former approach, the principal impediment to developing straightforward "cost/benefit ratios" for predictive decisionmaking is the lack of a common scale along which to order both costs and benefits (e.g., how are "years in a prison or mental hospital" to be compared with "rapes," "robberies," "murders," or "assaults" prevented?).

SUMMARY

The prediction of violent behavior has played an important role throughout legal history. It is currently used to assist in making a wide variety of legal decisions, from civil commitment to the imposition of the death penalty.

The term "violent behavior" appears preferable to "dangerousness." It can be defined as acts characterized by the application or overt threat of force which is likely to result in injury to people.

Three major criticisms are currently being made of the use of violence prediction by mental health professionals. It is claimed that violence cannot be predicted with any satisfactory level of accuracy and that any attempt to do so violates the civil liberties of the persons subject to prediction. As well, many believe that the societal protection rationale underlying the prediction of violent behavior is at variance with the traditional helping role of the mental health professions.

These criticisms involve several separable moral and political issues that a society must face in making any decisions on predictive grounds. These issues concern how the criterion of violence is defined, which items to include in reaching a predictive judgment, how likely violence must be to justify preventive action, and the nature of the preventive action that is to be taken. The moral status of any prediction, it is argued, will vary along these dimensions.

The actual process of making a clinical prediction of violent behavior is the subject of the next chapter.

NOTE

1. NY Criminal Procedure Law Section 730.50 (1971). This section is no longer in effect. It was found unconstitutional in 1974 in *People ex rel Anonymous* v. *Waugh*, 76 Misc. 2d 879, 351 N.Y.S. 2d 594 (Sup. Ct. 1974).

Chapter 2

THE CLINICAL PREDICTION PROCESS IN THEORY AND IN PRACTICE

How does one go about the task of predicting future behavior? Before a description of the prediction process, several concepts must be considered. They are (1) predictor and criterion variables; (2) outcomes of positive and negative prediction; (3) decision rules; and (4) base rates.

CORE CONCEPTS IN PREDICTION

PREDICTOR AND CRITERION VARIABLES

The prediction process requires that a person be assessed at two points in time. At Time One, he or she is placed into certain categories that are believed, for whatever reason, to relate to the behavior one is interested in predicting. If one is interested in predicting how well a person will do in college, the categories might be "grades in high school," "letters from teachers" (rated in some way such as "very good," "good," and "poor"), and "quality of the essay written for the application" (perhaps scored on a 1 to 10 scale). These are all *predictor variables,* categories consisting of different levels that are presumed to be relevant to what is being predicted. For violent behavior, the predictor variables might include "frequency of past violent acts," "age," or "degree of impulse control."

At some specified time in the future, Time Two, one performs another assessment of the person to ascertain whether he or she has or has not done what was predicted. This entails assessing the person on one or more *criterion variables.* For predicting "success" in college, the criterion variables might be "college grades," "class rank," or "whether or not the person got a job in the field he or she wanted" (scored simply as "yes" or "no"). For violent behavior, the criterion variables may include "self-report," "arrest" or "conviction" for certain crimes that are defined as violent, or involuntary commitment as "dangerous to others." They could also include professional or peer ratings of "aggressive behavior" or scores on psychological tests of aggression.

One major difficulty with the prediction of violence as it is practiced is that the clinician rarely has the chance to perform this assessment of the criterion variables at Time Two, since people are usually detained in a prison or mental hospital on the basis of how they score on the predictor variables at Time One. This, as we shall see, deprives the clinician of knowing whether the predictor variables *actually* relate to the criterion or are erroneously *assumed* to relate to it. This is one major reason why the prediction of violence is so much less precise than the prediction of the weather, for example. Each day's weather is the easily measured criterion for the previous day's prediction and provides the *feedback* necessary to make adjustments in the predictor variables.

OUTCOME OF POSITIVE AND NEGATIVE PREDICTIONS

There are four statistical outcomes that can occur when one is faced with making a prediction of any kind of future behavior. Table 1 displays these outcomes. One can either predict that the behavior, in this case, violence, *will occur* ("Yes") or that it *will not occur* ("No"). At the end of some specified time period, one observes whether the predicted behavior actually *has occurred* ("Yes") or *has not occurred* ("No").

TABLE 1 Four possible outcomes of predictive decisions

Predicted behavior	Actual behavior: Yes	Actual behavior: No.
Yes	true positive	false positive
No	false negative	true negative

If one predicts that violence will occur and later finds that, indeed, it has occurred, the prediction is called a *True Positive.* One has made a positive prediction, and it turned out to be correct or true. Likewise, if one predicts that violence will not occur and it in fact does not, the prediction is called a *True Negative,* since one has made a negative prediction of violence and it turned out to be true. These, of course, are the two outcomes one wishes to maximize in making predictions.

There are also two kinds of mistakes that can be made. If one predicts that violence *will* occur and it does *not,* the outcome is called a *False Positive.* One made a positive prediction of violence, and it turned out to be incorrect or false. In practice, this kind of mistake usually means that a person has been unnecessarily detained to prevent an act of violence that would not have occurred in any event. If one predicts that violence will *not* occur, and it does occur, the outcome is called a *False Negative.* In practice, this kind of mistake often means that someone who is not detained, or who is released from detention, commits an act of violence in the community. These two outcomes, obviously, are what predictors of violence try to minimize.

DECISION RULES

Decision rules are "guidelines for the handling of uncertainty" (American Psychiatric Association 1974, p. 26). They involve choosing a "cutting score" on some predictive scale, above which one predicts for the purpose of intervention that an event "will" happen. A cutting score is simply a particular point on some objective or subjective scale. When one sets a thermostat at 68°, for example, one is establishing a "cutting score" for the operation of a heating unit. When the temperature goes below 68°, the heat comes on, and when it goes above 68°, the heat goes off. In the treatment of cancer, as another example, one might decide that if tests show that a patient has a 20 percent chance of having cancer, it is best to operate. The decision rule or cutting score would then be a 20 percent probability—more than that you operate; less than that you don't. The "beyond a reasonable doubt" standard of proof in the criminal law is a cutting score for the degree of certainty a juror must have in order to vote for conviction. Conviction is to occur only if doubt is nonexistent or "unreasonable."

In civil law, on the other hand, the jurors generally need only decide which of two parties to a suit has the "preponderance of the evidence" on his or her side. Reasonable doubts can still remain. In the prediction of violent behavior for the purpose of invoking civil commitment, as another example, one could set the cutting score at "more likely than not" (or 51 percent likely) to be violent (Mental Health Law Project 1977). Any prediction falling short of this cutting score would not qualify for commitment, and any prediction meeting or exceeding it would. Clearly the cutting score can be set anywhere and can vary with the purpose and consequence of the prediction (one might, as noted in chapter 1, want a lower cutting score for short-term than for long-term commitment, for example).

Where the cutting score is set will determine the ratio of true to false positives. If the cutting score is set very low (e.g., "more violence-potential than the average citizen"), there will be many true positives, but many false positives also. If it is set very high (e.g., 90 percent likely), there will be fewer false positives, but fewer true positives as well.

It should be noted that the cutting score also determines the ratio of true positives and true negatives predicted and, therefore, the *absolute number* of successful predictions. If the decision rule is such that the cutting score is set very high, one will correctly identify most of the people who will not be violent, but at the expense of missing many of those who will be. Likewise, if the cutting score is low, one will correctly identify most of the people who will be violent, but at the cost of misidentifying many who would be safe.

It was argued previously that the choice of a decision rule is a political, rather than a professional, choice and that by all means the rule should be made explicit.

BASE RATES

The term "base rate" simply refers to the proportion of people in some population during a specified period of time who fall into the criterion category that is to be predicted. The time frame can be a matter of days or weeks or as long as one desires.

Table 2 presents the base rates for arrest for violent crime for the United States population in 1977 (Webster 1978). No comparable base rate for civil commitment as "dangerous to others" is available.

It is clear from the table, of course, that different subgroups of the population have different base rates of arrest for violent behavior. Males are arrested for violent crime nine times more frequently than females, for example. Yet, with the possible exception of that small group of persons with a history of chronic violent behavior—five or more offenses (Wolfgang 1978)—the base rate of violence in any population subgroup so far identified is low. It is not low by moral standards, since even one murder in a large population is tragic, but low purely in statistical terms. The concept of base rates is considered in detail later in this chapter.

THE CLINICAL PREDICTION PROCESS IN THEORY

Megargee (1976) has presented a model of the clinical process for the prediction of violent behavior. As have many others (e.g., Mischel, 1968, 1973), he categorized the relevant predictor variables as "personality" factors, "situational" factors, and interactions between the two.

TABLE 2 Arrest rate for violent crimes in the United States in 1977, per 100,000

	Murder	*Rape*	*Robbery*	*Assult*	*Total violent crimes*
Total U.S. population	9.0	13.5	64.2	116.0	202.7
Gender					
Male	14.8	25.8	114.5	194.9	350.0
Female	2.5	0.3	9.2	28.7	40.7
Race					
White	4.3	7.0	27.0	70.7	109.1
Black	35.5	49.7	284.4	349.9	719.6
Age					
15 years	6.4	18.5	187.5	158.7	371.0
18 years	20.0	37.6	259.4	262.4	577.4
21 years	21.7	38.2	175.6	263.2	498.7
30-34 years	14.1	19.1	50.3	166.7	250.3
40-44 years	8.7	8.2	15.7	108.7	141.3
50-54 years	4.7	2.9	4.8	52.3	64.6
Location					
Urban	19.4	26.9	170.9	180.4	397.5
Suburban	5.5	10.0	38.0	92.3	145.9
Region					
Northeast	5.9	13.2	83.7	117.3	220.1
North Central	7.8	11.6	52.3	59.5	131.2
Southern	11.7	14.5	53.2	137.1	216.5
Western	9.5	14.8	76.8	154.7	255.8

Obtained or computed from the Uniform Crime Reports (Webster 1978) and Bureau of the Census (1978).

PERSONALITY FACTORS

According to Megargee, three kinds of personality factors need to be assessed: *motivation, internal inhibition,* and *habit strength.*

Motivation

Following Buss (1961), Megargee distinguishes between "angry aggression" and "instrumental aggression" in the assessment of motivation. Angry aggression is motivated by a desire to harm someone and is reinforced by the victim's pain. Instrumental aggression is a means to some other end and has other reinforcements (e.g., shooting a guard to get at money in a bank). "Of course, both types of motivation may be mixed, as in the case of an angry parent who spanks a child partly to help socialize that child and partly to ventilate his or her own feelings" (p. 7).

Inhibition

Internal inhibitions are personal taboos against engaging in violent behavior. When inhibitions exceed motivation, violence will not occur. Inhibitions may vary by the type of target (e.g., one may be more inhibited from punching one's boss than from punching a stranger), and by the type of act (e.g., one may not be inhibited from throwing a punch but still be inhibited from using a knife or gun). Inhibitions can be lowered by alcohol or other drugs. Megargee (1976, p. 8) also notes that "some extremely violent people are characterized by excessive inhibitions. In such individuals, suppressed instigation to aggression apparently summated to the point where the massive inhibitions were overwhelmed" (see Megargee 1973 for a review of research on the Overcontrolled-Hostility Scale of the MMPI).

Habit

Habit strength in this context is simply the extent to which violent behavior has been reinforced in the past. The more instrumental violence has been in the past in obtaining money, peer approval, or sex, for example, the more the strength of violent "habits."

SITUATIONAL FACTORS

Situational factors are held by Megargee to be as important as personality ones:

> These include immediate specific factors such as the availability of a weapon, the presence of onlookers, and the behavior of a potential

victim, but more pervasive situational variables such as the level of frustration in the environment, or the social approval of violence in a particular subculture should also be considered (p. 9).

The topic of situational variables is pursued more fully in chapter 4.

INTERACTIONS

A mental health professional predicting violence must not simply assess how someone scores on the personality and situational variables chosen. It is also necessary to determine how the personality and situational variables *interact* with each other. A certain type of situation may increase the probability of violence for an individual with one type of personality and decrease it for an individual of another personality type. Toch (1969) views the interaction between personality variables and factors related to the *victim* as crucial to whether or not violence occurs:

> The violence-provoking incident typically consists of several stages: first, there is the classification of the other person as an object or a threat; second, there is some action based on this classification; third, the other person may act—if he has the chance—to protect his integrity. At this juncture, the violent incident reaches its point of no return. The initial stance of the violence-prone person makes violence probable; his first moves increase the probability of violence; the reaction of the victim converts probability into certainty (p. 184).

It should be noted, too, that "personality" and "situation" are not independent. Certain personalities seek out certain situations. Alternatively put, certain situations seem to draw certain personalities into them (Wicker 1972). If a bar gets a reputation as a place where fights frequently break out, some old customers will be repulsed and some new ones attracted. The bar situation will thus become more violent because it will be filled with more violent persons. As Endler and Magnusson (1976, p. 958) have put it:

> Not only is the individual's behavior influenced by significant features of the situations he or she encounters but the person also selects the situations in which he or she performs, and subsequently affects the character of these situations.

More generally, there may be much *overlap* among predictor items of either the personality or situational sort in terms of their ability to predict violence (in statistical terms, they may account for common variance). In this case, one cannot simply add together all the predictor variables to arrive at a total "score" for violence potential, since the items are not independent. For example, assume being poor is related to committing violence and being unemployed is also related to committing violence (see chapter 4). If one were asked to predict violence in a person who is both poor and unemployed, one could not add the "plus" for being poor with the "plus" for being unemployed, since being poor and being unemployed are *themselves correlated.* More unemployed than employed people are poor, and vice versa. One would want to know how much *new* (i.e., independent) information is conveyed by knowing one factor when we already know the other.

The Task Force on Clinical Aspects of the Violent Individual of the American Psychiatric Association (1974), while not recommending any one organized examination for predicting violent behavior, urged that a candid and extensive interview be undertaken.

> Questions about the violent patient's history should be frank and direct much as though one were questioning the suicide patient. The patient should be asked how much he has thought about violence, what he has done about it, what weapons does he have, what preparations he has made, how close he has come to being violent, and what is the most violent thing he has done. Corroborative data from a spouse, relative, or friend is sometimes necessary in problem cases (p. 11).

The Task Force also noted that suicidal patients should be evaluated for potential violence to others. "The patient may consider, for example, killing his family prior to killing himself, and his hopelessness may signal serious risk" (p. 13).

THE CLINICAL PREDICTION PROCESS IN PRACTICE

How do psychiatrists and psychologists actually go about predicting whether an individual will be violent? Numerous recent studies have examined the prediction process.

Dix (1976) observed professional staff meetings at Atascadero State Hospital in California concerned with whether given patients could be predicted to be "dangerous" and thus be recommended to stay in the hospital or could be predicted "nondangerous" and thus be released into the community. All the patients had been committed as "mentally disordered sex offenders." He concluded that eight factors entered into the staff's predictions:

1. *Acceptance of guilt and personal responsibility for offense.* The staff regarded as essential to nondangerousness that the patient admit commission of the offense, its seriousness, and personal responsibility for it.
2. *Development of ability to articulate resolution of stress-producing situations.* The staff regarded the prior conduct of many of the offenders as caused by their inability to deal with stressful life situations in an acceptable manner. When the manner in which such stressful situations arose was identified, the staff regarded it as essential that the patient be able to articulate a reasonable resolution of these matters. A relatively common indicator of continued dangerousness was an inability to deal with anger in a socially acceptable manner . . .
3. *Fantasies.* In relatively few cases was there–or at least did the staff elicit–evidence that the patient experienced fantasies in which he engaged in the conduct upon which the initial determination of dangerousness was based. But in those exceptional cases where such information was elicited, it was regarded as extremely important evidence of continued dangerousness.

4. *Behavior during hospitalization.* Significance was attached to the patient's behavior during hospitalization, but there seemed to be recognition that this was relatively unreliable, given the difference between the structured environment of the hospital and the conditions in which the patient would find himself after he is released.
5. *Duration of institutionalization.* Although indefinite therapeutic institutionalization is theoretically based on the assumption that the duration of institutionalization should depend on the person's condition rather than upon the activity engaged in, the staff did appear to be influenced by the amount of time spent in the facility. There was some indication that particular staff members regarded persons convicted of serious crimes as having to spend a certain "minimum" period in the institution.
6. *Achievement of maximum benefit from hospitalization.* The staff's decision in a number of cases seemed to be significantly influenced by the belief that the patient had reached maximum benefit from hospitalization or, conversely, that he would benefit from further exposure to institutional programs.
7. *Change in community circumstances.* The inference that "dangerousness" can be as much a function of the situation to which a person will be released as the characteristics of the person himself was demonstrated by those cases in which the staff's perception of the patient's continued dangerousness was affected by the attitude of those with whom he would live if released . . . Conversely, a person became no longer dangerous because of a change in the situation to which he would be released, without regard to whether his own psychological condition had undergone "change."
8. *Seriousness of the anticipated conduct.* To some extent, the staff's decision was affected by what they perceived as the seriousness of the conduct in which the subject might engage if released. Less serious conduct required a somewhat greater 'danger' to render the patient 'dangerous' than did conduct which the staff perceived as relatively more serious (p. 334ff.)

Many of the factors noted by Dix have been observed by other investigators. Williams and Miller (1977, p. 248), for example, found that in making predictions mental health professionals "attach considerable weight to the patient's mental status and perceived guilt or remorse." Aggressive fantasies have been stressed by many investigators. Skodol and Karasu (1978), examining 367 patients in the psychiatric emergency admitting unit of Bronx Municipal Hospital, predicted 62 cases (17 percent) to be violent. Over half of these patients had aggressive fantasies, with family members being the victims in 58 percent of the cases. In 77 percent of the cases in which the patients admitted to actively considering violence, the victims were family members. Thus, they contend, "the explicit statement of an intention to do harm is, in fact, a serious situation. When a family member is the target, we have found that the danger is increased" (p. 204). They also note, however, that the "assault that psychiatrists see under acute conditions is frequently unaccompanied by admitted hostile or aggressive ideation. The patients either are unable, because of defensive structuring, or unwilling to confront aggressive impulses before they spill over into acting out behavior" (p. 204). MacDonald (1967) reported that of 100 hospitalized patients who threatened to kill, only 7 had actually done so within 5 years. It is impossible to know, however, how many of these persons would have killed had they not been hospitalized.

Pfohl (1977) observed 37 psychologists, psychiatrists, and social workers perform prediction examinations on 130 patients at the Lima State Hospital for the Criminally Insane in Ohio. In nearly all cases, a past history of violence was an assumed prerequisite for viewing a patient as dangerous. Two factors qualified this prerequisite, however. One was that more significance was assigned to recent violence than to violence in the remote past, with the definition of remote varying across the examiners.

> A second qualifier to the criterion of past violence occurred in cases where teams noted the presence of "dangerous delusions.' Such delusions were most frequently said to represent paranoid construction in which patients had much self-investment . . . [S]uch delusions were often assumed to be predictive of dangerousness despite the absence of any history of violent acts (p. 84).

In this regard, the American Psychiatric Association Task Force (1974) agreed that "Delusional patients with violent fantasies should be taken seriously" (p. 13).

It is important to distinguish between the factors clinicians *believe* they are using—correctly or incorrectly—to predict violent behavior and the factors that actually appear to influence their decisions. Cocozza and Steadman (1978) examined the reasons given by psychiatrists when they predicted violence in defendants found incompetent to stand trial. The only factor that statistically related to whether psychiatrists predicted violence was the type of crime the defendant was charged with. Almost three-fourths of those charged with violent crimes were predicted to be violent, while only 30 percent of those accused of crimes such as forgery and gambling were predicted violent. Yet only 11 percent of the reasons given by psychiatrists to justify their predictions concerned the type of crime with which the person was charged.

Analogously, Konečni, Mulcahy and Ebbesen (1980) studied the determination by psychiatrists and courts of whether a person was a "mentally disordered sex offender" (MDSO), a designation that involves a prediction of violent behavior. While many reasons were given by the psychiatrists for their findings, one factor—prior conviction of the defendant for sexual offenses—virtually determined the psychiatric predictions and the ultimate judicial determinations. "Indeed," they noted, "to the extent that psychiatrists are basing their recommendations on such an easily observed and agreed upon factor as prior sex-related criminal record, their usefulness in the processing of persons suspected of being MDSO's would appear rather limited."

COMMON CLINICAL ERRORS IN PREDICTION

There are many mistakes that a psychiatrist or psychologist can make in predicting violent behavior. He or she can mis-score a test, forget to ascertain a relevant fact, or simply be unaware of the research findings in the area. Several sources of error, however, appear to occur so routinely in the prediction of violent behavior, even by generally competent clinicians, that it is worthwhile to single them out for special attention. The four most common "blind spots" in the clinical prediction of violent behavior appear to be: (1) lack of specificity in defining the criterion; (2) ignoring statistical base rates; (3) relying on illusory correlations; and (4) failing to incorporate situational or environmental information.

LACK OF SPECIFICITY IN DEFINING THE CRITERION

The difficulty of specifying an acceptable definition of violence or "dangerousness" has already been addressed. The point here is that one cannot even hope to predict what has not been defined. *Some* specification of a criterion–even one as simple as the FBI's four "violent index crimes" of murder, forcible rape, robbery, and aggravated assault–is essential if prediction is to succeed.

It should be clear that the more inclusive the definition, the greater the predictive accuracy: Large targets are easier to hit than small ones. The data bear out this axiom. One attempt to predict "assaultive behavior" had 16 percent true positives when the criterion was defined as "homicide, all assaults, attempted murder, battery, forcible rape and attempt to rape," 22.6 percent true positives when the criterion was expanded to include "other sex offenses and kidnapping," and 53 percent true positives when assaultive behavior was construed still more loosely to encompass "all of the above plus robbery, all sex offenses, weapon offenses and disturbing the peace" (cited in Halatyn 1975). While predictive accuracy is indeed increased as definitions of violence expand, there comes a point at which it is arguable whether one is studying violence or simply any kind of lawbreaking. Including "disturbing the peace" as violence, for example, would seem to stretch the concept to its breaking point.

A good deal of the ambiguity found in current prediction research may reflect the fact that mental health professionals are often unclear about just what they are predicting will happen. Thus, Forst (1977) found the lowest rate of commitment as a Mentally Disordered Sex Offender in the California county that limited the definition of "dangerous" behavior to physically assaultive acts and the highest rate of commitment in the county that included "psychological danger" in its criterion.

If a psychiatrist or psychologist considers "writing a bad check" to be sufficiently dangerous behavior to justify institutionalization to prevent its occurrence (*Overholser* v. *Russell* 1960), and if the validation researcher limits his or her definition of dangerousness to the FBI violent index crimes, it would not be surprising to find overprediction reported. Rather than overprediction, however, this would more properly be a case of unsynchronized definitions. Even if the predictions were perfectly accurate–if those predicted to write bad checks actually wrote them–the follow-up researcher using a less inclusive definition of violence would report them as "false positives."

IGNORING STATISTICAL BASE RATES

Probably the most common and surely the most significant error made by clinicians in predicting violent behavior is the ignoring of information regarding the statistical base rate of violence in the population in question.

The base rate, it will be recalled, is simply the statistical prevalence of violent behavior in a given group, that is, the frequency with which violence is committed in a given time period (usually 1 year).

For at least the past 25 years (Meehl and Rosen 1955), it has been known that it is virtually impossible to predict any "low base rate" event without at the same time erroneously pointing the finger at many "false positives." Livermore et al. (1968) provide a telling example of this dilemma.

> Assume that one person out of a thousand will kill. Assume also that an exceptionally accurate test is created which differentiates with 95 percent effectiveness those who will kill from those who will not. If 100,000 people were tested, out of the 100 who would kill, 95 would

be isolated. Unfortunately, out of the 99,900 who would not kill, 4,995 people would also be isolated as potential killers. In these circumstances, it is clear that we could not justify incarcerating all 5,090 people. If, in the criminal law, it is better that ten guilty men go free than that one innocent man suffer, how can we say in the civil commitment area that it is better that 54 harmless people be incarcerated lest one dangerous man be free? (p. 84)

Ideally, the "best" population on which to apply clinical predictions of violence is one with a base rate of 50 percent, since in this population the potential effect of the predictions in distinguishing the violent from the nonviolent will be maximized (Hanley 1979). As the base rate differs substantially from 50 percent, clinical differentiation becomes progressively more difficult. If 90 percent of a group will be nonviolent, the best prediction in the individual case is to predict them all nonviolent. If another group has a base rate of 90 percent for violent behavior, the most accurate prediction would be to predict them all violent.

It should be recalled, however, that overall accuracy is not the only factor involved in prediction. One may wish to *weigh* different kinds of errors differently. Thus, in mental health law (e.g., civil commitment), it appears legally acceptable to weigh a false negative (e.g., a released patient who injures someone) more heavily than a false positive (e.g., a safe person erroneously hospitalized as dangerous). In criminal law, as Livermore et al. noted, the reverse appears true.

It is clear that *knowledge of the appropriate base rate is the most important single piece of information necessary to make an accurate prediction.* This makes Kahneman and Tversky's (1973) finding that people often ignore base rates in making predictions a matter of considerable concern.

Kahneman and Tversky found that people ignore base rates when case-specific information is present. Even when the case-specific information is highly unreliable, it appears to make people forget about base rates. When no case-specific information is present, however, people will, as they should, rely on base rates.

> Evidently, people respond differently when given no specific evidence and when given worthless evidence. When no specific evidence is given, the prior probabilities [i.e., base rates] are properly utilized; when worthless specific evidence is given, prior probabilities are ignored (p. 242).

Nisbett et al. (1976) provide an interesting example of how case-specific information can overwhelm knowledge about base rates:

> Let us suppose that you wish to buy a new car and have decided that on grounds of economy and longevity you want to purchase one of those solid, stalwart, middle class Swedish cars—either a Volvo or a Saab. As a prudent and sensible buyer, you go to *Consumer Reports,* which informs you that the consensus of their experts is that the Volvo is mechanically superior, and the consensus of the readership is that the Volvo has the better repair record. Armed with this information, you decide to go out and strike a bargain with the Volvo dealer before the week is out. In the interim, however, you go to a cocktail party where you announce this intention to an acquaintance. He reacts with disbelief and alarm: "A Volvo! You've got to be kidding. My brother-in-law had a Volvo. First, that fancy fuel injection computer thing went out. 250 bucks. Next he started having trouble with the rear end. Had to replace it. Then the transmission and the clutch. Finally he sold it in three years for junk (p. 129).

Logically, the case of the acquaintance's brother-in-law should simply add one more car to the thousands of cars which contributed to the base rates reported in *Consumer Reports* and therefore should have no appreciable effect on one's decision. Psychologically, however, the impact of the case-specific information far exceeds its statistical usefulness (Carroll 1979).

Shah (1978) has noted that an occupational hazard of the mental health professions appears to be a tendency to give too much weight to case information at the expense of base rates.

> In fact, one might even wonder about the extent to which professional training and related clinical experiences tend to socialize (or

even to indoctrinate) clinicians into practices in which exaggerated and possibly erroneous credence is given to specific information about persons in the form of various "clinical" and "pathognomonic" signs, even though the base-rates involved may be low and the reliability of certain "signs" quite poor (p. 164).

Shapiro (1977), in this regard, studied the use of clinical predictions in medicine. He noted the use of "anchoring" as a prediction strategy. "Anchoring" refers to using the base rate of a condition as one's first estimate of the probability of the condition's being present in the individual case. Subsequently, the clinician will use additional patient-specific information to individualize his or her probability estimate around this anchor point.

> Clearly, inaccuracy in prediction can be due either to use of an incorrect anchor point or to failure to individualize appropriately. Skill in these two aspects of prediction is acquired differently. A correct anchor-point probability may be obtained either through knowledge of the literature or by extensive clinical experience. Ability to individualize assessments to the unique characteristics of the patient is primarily a function of experience (p. 1512).

Shapiro's (1977) research showed that some physicians were poor predictors because they could not estimate base rates properly, and others, who could estimate base rates, were poor predictors because they could not individualize them in light of relevant case specific information. For further discussion of the "judgmental heuristics" involved in clinical prediction, see Kahneman and Tversky (1973), Tversky and Kahneman (1974), Ajzen (1977), and Shah (1978).

RELYING UPON ILLUSORY CORRELATIONS

An illusory correlation occurs when an observer reports that a correlation exists between two classes of events which, in fact, are not correlated or are correlated to a lesser degree or in the direction opposite to that reported (Chapman and Chapman 1969). In an ingenious experiment, Chapman and Chapman presented experienced mental health professionals with a series of responses of hypothetical patients to projective tests and paired these responses with statements about the symptoms reported by the patients. When asked what relationships they had observed in the material presented to them, the clinicians responded with relationships that "made sense" in terms of their prior biases, rather than in terms of what they had actually seen. For example, a response emphasizing the eyes in a figure drawing was consistently associated with suspiciousness and paranoia, and Rorshach responses pertaining to the buttocks were consistently associated with male homosexuality, *even when the correlations did not exist in reality.*

Sweetland (1972) has demonstrated how this phenomenon influences the assessment of dangerousness. Psychiatrists were surveyed to determine which personality traits they considered to be most characteristic of dangerous persons. Their six most frequent responses were: "often acts on impulse," "has no conscience whatsoever," "is addicted to heroin," "is utterly irresponsible," "fears that people are out to get him," and "resents even the slightest criticism." Following this, naive subjects were asked to examine personality descriptions which were made up of these characteristics and which were paired with the diagnoses "dangerous" or "nondangerous." In one condition of this study, there was no relationship between the items designated by the psychiatrists as indicating a dangerous person and the diagnosis with which these items were paired. Subjects were asked after the presentation to describe what they had observed. The results indicated that, even when there was no relationship, the subjects responded as if they had observed a relationship in the materials. They consistently recalled that certain of the characteristics had appeared more frequently with the diagnosis of "dangerous," when, in fact, they were not correlated. These systematic errors of observation were consistent with the subjects' prior expectations about which characteristics implied dangerousness.

Hartogs (1970), for example, lists 48 alleged predictors of violence, including "lack of family interest, love, support, or acceptance" (p. 335) and "conflict over basic identity" (p. 333). Commenting on Hartogs' criteria, Diamond (1974, p. 443) states:

> It would be difficult for an objective observer to take such claims seriously if such pseudo-scientific descriptions had not been reiterated so often that they have become part of the accepted mythology of clinical practice. I am sure that many patients have been labelled as dangerous and have been institutionalized for long periods of time upon the basis of such flimsy clinical criteria.

FAILING TO INCORPORATE ENVIRONMENTAL INFORMATION

Since many of the individuals involved in violence-prediction efforts have been mental health professionals or others who have adopted a "mental health ideology," almost all of the variables that have been investigated as predictors of violence have been dispositional variables. That is, they have referred to fixed or relatively enduring attributes or traits of the person under study, such as age, sex, race, prior criminal record, or psychiatric history and diagnosis. This reliance upon dispositional variables or personal traits has characterized not only the prediction of violence but the prediction of all types of behavior. The result has been the same in each case: low correlations between predictor and criterion variables (Mischel 1968; cf. Bem and Allen 1974). In this regard, Arthur (1971), reviewing studies of the prediction of military performance, has stated that a prediction "sound barrier" exists, since "no matter how much information about the individual one adds to the predictive equation, one cannot bring the correlation coefficient between individual characteristics and prediction criteria much above about .40" (p. 544). This "sound barrier" remains unbroken by research on the prediction of violence.

An alternative to the dispositional or trait perspective in the mental health fields has arisen that offers a possible source of previously overlooked variables to include in prediction research. While the seeds of the ecological perspective on human behavior have been planted for some time (e.g., Park 1925), it is only recently that this approach has been taken seriously in psychology (Kelly 1966; Moos and Insel 1973; Stokols 1977).

The ecological or environmental perspective on human behavior derives in part from a new appreciation of the dictum that behavior is a joint function of characteristics of the person and characteristics of the environment with which he or she interacts (Lewin et al. 1939). Until recently, psychological and psychiatric research had focused almost solely on dispositional or person variables. The ecological approach attempts to right this imbalance by an emphasis upon situational or environmental variables as they interact with personal characteristics. While environmental research of relevance to the topic of violent behavior has been initiated (Newman 1972), there has as yet been no empirical attempt to apply the ecological or environmental perspective to the problem of the prediction of violent behavior. This is despite the fact that there is coming to be widespread agreement with Moos' statement (1975) that "to adequately predict individual aggressive behavior, one must know something about the environment in which the individual is functioning" (p. 13).

Chapter 4 attempts to present some suggestions on how situational or environmental factors might be incorporated into the clinical prediction process. It is interesting to note that, while researchers have been slow to explore situational aspects of violent behavior, their importance has not escaped sensitive clinicians (e.g., Meehl 1954). Guttmacher (1967, p. 27) has noted that difficulties with prediction are "due to the fact that one cannot anticipate with accuracy social situations which the released . . . patient will have to meet." Cohen, Groth, and Siegel (1978) also have expressed the importance of environmental factors:

> Clinical data show clearly that a person evaluated as high risk based on pre-release data may well be a false positive error if environmental factors are not included in the prediction. If the released offender enters a stable, supportive home in a concerned community, and undertakes a self-selected job that provides financial support and personal gratification, his high risk evaluation may be inaccurate (p. 33).

SUMMARY

Several concepts facilitate understanding the process of predicting violent behavior. *Predictor variables* are the items one uses to to arrive at the prediction, such as demographic factors and scores on a clinical examination. *Criterion variables* are the acts one includes in the definition of what one is predicting, such as in the case of violent behavior, murder, robbery, rape, and assault.

The accepted framework for analyzing the accuracy of predictions includes four possible outcomes: A *True Positive* is a prediction of violence that later turns out to be correct, and a *True Negative* is a prediction of nonviolence that likewise is proven correct; a *False Positive* occurs when one predicts that violence will occur and it does not, and a *False Negative* occurs when one predicts nonviolence for a person who later becomes violent.

Whether preventive action is taken on the basis of a prediction of violence depends on the decision rule that has been adopted. A decision rule involves choosing a point on a scale of violence potential above which one predicts for the purpose of intervention that violence will occur. The choice of a decision rule–which, it is argued, is a political rather than a professional choice–will determine the proportion of accurate predictions and mistakes that will occur.

The most important single piece of information one can have in prediction violence is the *base rate* for violent behavior in the population with which one is dealing. The base rate is simply the proportion of people in the population who will commit a violent act in a given time period (e.g., the annual arrest rate for violent crimes for a given group).

The process of making a clinical prediction involves assessing a person on at least three general types of predictor variables, namely, personality factors, situational factors, and interactions between the two. Personality factors can be further subdivided into motivational factors, inhibiting factors, and the degree to which violent habits have been instrumental in obtaining rewards in the past. A good deal of overlap may exist between these various predictors.

Studies of the variables that psychiatrists and psychologists rely upon in predicting violent behavior reveal a variety of items, including acceptance of guilt and personal responsibility for violent acts committed, the ability to cope with anger and other stresses, violent fantasies, delusions and threats, institutional behavior, the length of institutionalization and its presumed benefit, a change in community circumstances, the seriousness of the anticipated violence, and whether or not the intended victims are family members. The existence of past violent behavior appears to be the best indicator of whether a mental health professional will predict violence in the future.

In the process of predicting violent behavior, clinicians appear prone to several types of systematic error, including vagueness as to what is being predicted, lack of attention to base rates of violent behavior, reliance upon erroneous predictor items, and a failure to take into account information regarding the environment in which the individual is to function.

Chapter 3

RESEARCH ON CLINICAL PREDICTION

This chapter reviews the research that exists on the ability of psychiatrists and psychologists to predict violent behavior and discusses the criticisms and limitations of that research.

CHILDHOOD PREDICTION OF ADULT VIOLENCE

There has been much writing, but little research, on the childhood precursors of adult violent behavior. The triad of enuresis, pyromania, and cruelty to animals (e.g., Hellman and Blackman 1966) is probably the most frequently cited set of predictors of this sort. One survey (Justice, Justice and Kraft 1974) reviewed 1,500 references to violence in psychiatric literature, interviewed over 750 professionals who dealt with violent persons, and retrospectively analyzed over 1,000 clinical cases to ascertain the most cited childhood predictors of adult violence. The authors reported that the four "early warning signs" were fighting, temper tantrums, school problems, and an inability to get along with others. The child, in other words, is indeed father or mother to the adult.

Based on discussions with large groups of psychiatrists and psychologists, Goldstein (1974) concluded that the "agreed upon" predictors of violence were "a childhood history of maternal deprivation, poor father identification, or both; nocturnal enuresis; possibly fire setting; violence toward animals; and brutalization by one or both parents" (p. 27). Diamond (1974) comments that the conclusion of the clinicians cited by Goldstein represents the sum total of our present "scientific" knowledge concerning predictive factors of murderous violence.

> Yet I have repeatedly found some, and sometimes all of these predictive factors, in individuals who have never committed even the slightest harmful act, let alone assault or murder. And I have examined offenders who have committed the extraordinarily brutal acts of great violence and lethality who possessed none of these factors. (Diamond 1974, p. 444.)

One of the most famous studies of the childhood correlates of later criminal behavior is *Unraveling Juvenile Delinquency,* published by Glueck and Glueck in 1950. While not concerned specifically with violent criminality, the Gluecks claimed that three factors—supervision by the mother, discipline by the mother, and cohesiveness of the family—were predictive of later crime in young adolescent boys. This research is among the most methodologically criticized in all of criminology, and there appears to be a consensus that the practical utility of the Glueck factors in predicting criminality is marginal at best.

Lefkowitz, Eron, Walder, and Huesman (1977) published the results of a longitudinal study entitled *Growing Up To Be Violent.* This research followed a sample of over 400 males and females in Columbia County, New York, from ages 8 to 19. They used peer ratings, parent ratings, self-report, and a personality test to measure "aggressive behavior." Lefkowitz and his coworkers found that "aggression at age 8 is the best predictor we have of aggression at age 19, irrespective of IQ, social class, or parents' aggressiveness" (p. 192). Several other variables, among them the father's upward social mobility, low identification of the child with his/her parents, and a preference on the part of boys for watching violent television programs, were statistically significant predictors of aggression at age 19. Boys who, in the third grade, preferred television programs such as "Gunsmoke" or "Have Gun, Will Travel" were rated by their peers 10 years later as three times as aggressive as boys who, in the third grade, preferred "Ozzie and Harriet," "I Love Lucy," or "Lawrence Welk." What is not clear from the study is why an 8-year-old boy would prefer "Lawrence Welk" to "Have Gun, Will Travel" in the first place.

McCord (1979) has reported on a 30-year follow-up of 201 boys who participated in the Cambridge-Sommerville Youth Project between 1939 and 1945. She found that 36 percent of the incidence of later violent criminality could be accounted for by childhood predictive factors. "The boys who lacked supervision, whose mothers lacked self-confidence, who had been exposed to parental conflict and to aggression were subsequently more convicted for personal crimes" (McCord, 1979, p. 1481).

In what has become the most influential criminological research of the past decade (Geis and Meier 1978), Wolfgang et al. (1972) obtained information on all boys born in Philadelphia in 1945 who lived there between their 10th and 18th birthdays. Of the 9,945 boys studied, 3,475, or 35 percent, had at least one recorded contact with the police by age 18. Wolfgang et al. found that the variables of race and socioeconomic status (SES) were most strongly associated with reported delinquency: 29 percent of the whites, but 50 percent of the nonwhites, and 26 percent of the higher SES, but 45 percent of the lower SES boys had an offense record.

"Chronic" offenders were defined as those who committed five or more violations. Six hundred and twenty-seven boys—6 percent of the sample and 18 percent of the total number of offenders—were responsible for over one-half of all offenses committed.

Chronic offenders in the cohort had a greater number of residential moves, lower IQ scores, a greater percentage classified as retarded, and fewer grades completed than did either the nonchronic or the one-time offenders, even when race and SES were held constant (p. 248).

Wolfgang (1977) has updated his research to include data on the subjects up to age 30. Only 5 percent of the subjects had an arrest record only as an adult (i.e., after age 18 but not before).

While most juvenile offenders (61 percent) avoid arrest upon reaching adulthood, the chances of being an adult offender are almost four times greater if one had a juvenile record than if one did not. While 6 percent of the sample were "chronic" offenders by age 18, 15 percent were chronic by age 30. The probability of future arrest varied directly with the probability of past arrest: The probability of a fifth arrest (for any crime not necessarily a violent one) given four "priors" was .80; the probability of an eleventh arrest given ten previous arrests was .90. The probability of a fifth *serious* (or "index") offense with four prior arrests was .36; the probability of an eleventh serious offense given ten previous arrests was .42.

During the juvenile years, the subjects reported committing 8 to 11 serious or index offenses for every time they were arrested. Adults admitted to between three and six offenses for each recorded act.

The main conclusion one could draw from the research on childhood predictors of adult violence is that the distinction between "childhood" and "adulthood" is not a particularly meaningful one in terms of violence prediction. The same factors (e.g., a history of past violence) appear to influence the occurrence of future violence regardless of age. Age is relevant to the extent that the earlier one begins a career of violence, the longer and more extensive that history may be, and as one enters the 30s, maturation processes become salient. The search for factors that "imprint" a violent disposition at an early age so far has produced results that are theoretically interesting but without much practical significance for prediction in the individual case.

OUTCOME STUDIES OF CLINICAL PREDICTION

There have been at least five studies published since 1972 attempting to validate the ability of psychiatrists and psychologists to predict violent behavior. Kozol et al. (1972) reported a 10-year study involving 592 male offenders, most of whom had been convicted of violent sex crimes. At the Massachusetts Center for the Diagnosis and Treatment of Dangerous Persons, each offender was examined independently by at least two psychiatrists, two psychologists, and a social worker. These clinical examinations, along with a full psychological test battery and "a meticulous reconstruction of the life history elicited from multiple sources—the patient himself, his family, friends, neighbors, teachers, employers, and court, correctional and mental hospital record" (p. 383) formed the data base for their predictions.

Of the 592 patients admitted to their facility for diagnostic observation, 435 were released. Kozol et al. recommended the release of 386 as nondangerous and opposed the release of 49 as dangerous (with the court deciding otherwise). During the 5-year follow-up period, 8 percent of those predicted not to be dangerous became recidivists by committing a serious assaultive act, and 34.7 percent of those predicted to be dangerous committed such an act.

While the assessment of dangerousness by Kozol and his colleagues appears to have some validity, the problem of false positives stands out. Sixty-five percent of the individuals identified as dangerous did not, in fact, commit a dangerous act. Despite the extensive examining, testing, and data gathering they undertook, Kozol et al. were wrong in two out of every three predictions of discovered violence (cf., Monahan 1973; Kozol, Boucher, and Garofalo 1973).

The Patuxent Institution in Maryland was similar in purpose to Kozol's Massachusetts Center. Data are available on its first 10 years of operation (State of Maryland 1973). Four hundred and twenty-one patients, each of whom received at least 3 years of treatment at Patuxent, are considered. The psychiatric staff opposed the release of 286 of these patients on the grounds that they were still dangerous (with the court releasing them anyway). The staff recommended the release of 135 patients as safe (with the court concurring). The criterion measure was any new offense (*not* necessarily violent) appearing on the FBI reports of ex-patients during the first 3 years after their release.

Of those patients released by the court against staff advice, the recidivism rate was 46 percent if patients had been released directly from the hospital and 39 percent if a "conditional release experience" had been imposed. Of those patients released on the staff's recommendation and continued for outpatient treatment on parole, 7 percent recidivated. Thus, after at least 3 years of observation and treatment, between 54 and 61 percent of the patients predicted by the staff to be dangerous actually were found to be safe. As with the Kozol et al. (1972) study, some predictive validity does seem to accrue to the psychiatric predictions (7 percent recidivism, compared with 39 to 46 percent recidivism). Still, the majority of those patients predicted dangerous were actually not discovered to be criminal in any sense. In addition, it is possible that variables other than psychiatric ones accounted for the differential recidivism rates. Those who remained until the staff considered them "cured" were older than those released by the courts against staff advice (30- versus 23-years-old). Their lower rate of recidivism may in part be attributed to their being older.

A more recent and much more sophisticated evaluation of Patuxent by Steadman (1977) concluded that "the rearrest rate for both violent offenses and all offenses of all those released to the street with Patuxent approval vary much less from those of all relevant comparison groups than prior reports have demonstrated" (p. 206). For example, the arrest rate for *violent* crime over a 3-year period for those inmates recommended by the staff for release (i.e., those predicted not dangerous) was 31 percent, while the comparable rate for those predicted violent by the staff but released by the court was 41 percent. This 10-percent difference between the groups predicted to be violent and to be safe is much more modest than the 32- to 39-percent difference claimed in the earlier research. (see Gordon 1977 for a contrasting view of this study). Based partially on these new research findings, the Maryland legislature has abolished the "Defective Delinquent" statute under which the Patuxent program operated.

In 1966, the U.S. Supreme Court held that Johnnie Baxstrom had been denied equal protection of the law by being detained beyond his maximum sentence in an institution for the criminally insane without the benefit of a new hearing to determine his current dangerousness (*Baxstrom* v. *Herold* 1966). Baxstrom had received a prison sentence, and, before it was to expire, he was diagnosed as mentally disordered and transferred to a hospital for the criminally insane, where he was kept past the date his sentence had expired. The court ruled that he must be released or at least granted a civil commitment hearing at which the State would have to prove his "dangerousness." The ruling resulted in the transfer of nearly 1,000 persons "reputed to be some of the most dangerous mental patients in the state (of New York)" from hospitals for the criminally insane to civil mental hospitals (Steadman 1972). It also provided an excellent opportunity for naturalistic research on the validity of the psychiatric predictions of dangerousness upon which the extended detentions were based.

There has been an extensive follow-up program on the Baxstrom patients (Steadman and Cocozza 1974). Researchers found that the level of violence experienced in the civil mental hospitals was much less than had been feared, that the civil hospitals adapted well to the massive transfer of patients, and that the Baxstrom patients were treated the same as the civil patients. Only 20 percent of the Baxstrom patients were assaultive to persons in the civil hospital or the community at any time during the 4 years following their transfer. Furthermore, only 3 percent of Baxstrom patients were sufficiently dangerous to be returned to a hospital for the criminally insane during 4 years after the decision (Steadman and Halfon 1971). Steadman and Keveles (1972) followed 121 Baxstrom patients who had been released into the community (i.e., discharged from both the criminal and civil mental hospitals). During an average of 2½ years of freedom, only 9 of the 121 patients (8 percent) were convicted of a crime, and only one of those convictions was for a violent act. The researchers found that a Legal Dangerousness Scale (LDS) was most predictive of violent behavior. The scale was composed of four items: presence of juvenile record, number of previous arrests, presence of convictions for violent crimes, and severity of the original Baxstrom offense. In subsequent analyses, Cocozza and Steadman (1974) found that the only other variable highly related to subsequent criminal activity was age (under 50-years-old). In one study, 17 of 20 Baxstrom patients who were arrested for a violent crime when released into the community were under 50 and had a score of 5 or above on the 15-point Legal Dangerousness Scale. Yet the authors concluded:

> For every patient who was under 50 years old and who had an LDS score of 5 or more and who was dangerous, there were at least two who were not. Thus, using these variables we get a false positive ratio of 2 to 1 . . . Despite the significant relationship between the two variables of age and LDS score and dangerous behavior if we were to attempt to use this information for statistically predicting dangerous behavior our best strategy would still be to predict that none of the patients would be dangerous (pp. 1013-1014).

Note that in referring to the "best strategy" on prediction, Cocozza and Steadman mean the strategy that would reduce the *total* error rate (i.e., false positives plus false negatives). As mentioned previously, however, some kinds of errors may be much more important than other kinds, and the "best" strategy should take into account the relative "weights" or "costs" of different kinds of mistakes.

The Supreme Court's Baxstrom decision prompted a similar group of "mentally disordered offenders" in Pennsylvania to petition successfully for release (*Dixon* v. *Pennsylvania* 1971). The results of the release of 438 patients have been reported by Thornberry and Jacoby (1979) and are remarkably similar to those reported by Steadman. Only 14 percent of the former patients were discovered to have engaged in behaviors injurious to other persons within 4 years after their release.

Finally, Cocozza and Steadman (1976) followed 257 indicted felony defendants found incompetent to stand trial in New York State in 1971 and 1972. All defendants were examined for a determination of dangerousness by two psychiatrists, with 60 percent being predicted to be dangerous and 40 percent not dangerous. Subjects were followed in the hospital and in the community (if they were eventually released) during a 3-year period. While those predicted to be dangerous were slightly but insignificantly more likely to be assaultive during their initial incompetency hospitalization than those predicted not to be dangerous (42 percent compared with 36 percent), this relationship was reversed for those rearrested for a crime after their release, with 49 percent of the dangerous group and 54 percent of the not-dangerous group rearrested. Predictive accuracy was poorest in the case of a rearrest for a violent crime, "perhaps the single most important indicator of the success of the psychiatric predictions." Only 14 percent of the dangerous group, compared with 16 percent of the not-dangerous group, were rearrested for violent offenses. While these data are susceptible to alternative interpretations involving the possibly confounding effects of treatment received during hospitalization (Monahan 1978), the authors believe that they constitute "the most definitive evidence available on the lack of expertise and accuracy of psychiatric predictions of dangerousness" and indeed represent "clear and convincing evidence of the inability of psychiatrists or of anyone else to accurately predict dangerousness."

These five studies are summarized in table 3.

If one takes into account that the 46 percent true positive rate reported in the first Patuxent study refers to *any* crimes, not necessarily violent ones, and discounts that figure accordingly, it would be fair to conclude that the "best" clinical research currently in existence indicates that *psychiatrists and psychologists are accurate in no more than one out of three predictions of violent behavior over a several-year period among institutionalized populations that had both committed violence in the past (and thus had high base rates for it) and who were diagnosed as mentally ill.*

A very different perspective on the research on "dangerousness" is put forward by Gordon (1977). According to him, "The error of the critics of predictability could be characterized as assuming the prediction in question is of dangerous behavior, when it is really of the probability of dangerous behavior. In the former case the prediction might seem poor, whereas in the latter case, it might be superb" (p. 251). Mental health professionals, in his view, do not predict that violent behavior *will* occur; rather, they predict that an individual has a certain propensity to act violently. Whether he or she actually *behaves* violently will depend upon whether chance factors—factors that the clinician cannot know about in advance—trigger these propensities. Thus, for example, an individual could be predicted to be "dangerous," if it were believed that he would assault someone who cast aspersions upon his masculinity. This person would be "dangerous," *even if it happened that no one ever triggered violent behavior* by casting such aspersions. "Whether or not a released inmate recidivates may depend on chance factors such as recalling something his therapist said at the moment of temptation or falling in with the right companions" (Gordon 1977, p. 234). What this means for Gordon is that "false positives"—people predicted to be "dangerous" but not later found to have committed violent acts—may have been just as "dangerous" as the "true positives" discovered to have committed violent behavior. It is only that the chance factors that elicited violence in the latter groups were fortuitously absent in the former.

The difficulty with this position is that it makes the accuracy of prediction impossible to test. The mental health professional cannot lose: If the person predicted to be "dangerous" is discovered to have committed a violent act, he or she can say "I told you so"; if the person is not found to have acted violently, the clinician has the retort, "It's just lucky that nobody has triggered this person's dangerousness yet."

It is true, as discussed in chapter 4, that situational or environmental factors can exert a great influence on the occurrence of violent behavior. To be meaningful in predictive terms, however, these environmental or situation factors would have to be specified at the time the prediction is made and not simply fobbed off as "chance." For example, it would be quite acceptable to say that a person has a 50 percent probability of being violent, if he goes back to his old friends and a 20 percent chance if he does not. To ascertain the probability of the person actually committing a violent act, the clinician would then have

TABLE 3 Validity studies of the clinical prediction of violent behavior

Study	*Percent true positive*	*Percent false positive*	*Percent true negative*	*Percent false negative*	*Number predicted violent*	*Number predicted nonviolent*	*Followup years*
Kozol et al. (1972)	34.7	65.3	92.0	8.0	49	386	5
Steadman and Cocozza (1974)	20.0	80.0	–	–	967	–	4
Cocozza and Steadman (1976)	14.0	86.0	84.0	16.0	154	103	3
Steadman (1977)	41.3	58.7	68.8	31.2	46	106	3
Thornberry and Jacoby (1979)	14.0	86.0	–	–	438	–	4

to make a separate judgment on how likely the individual was to get back to his old friends. It would not be acceptable, it seems to me, for the clinician to say that the person has a 50 percent probability of being dangerous "under certain circumstances" and then not say what these situations were or how likely they were to occur.

PSYCHOLOGICAL TESTS

In a comprehensive review of the use of psychological tests to predict violence, Megargee (1970, p. 145) concluded that no test has been developed "which will adequately *post*dict, let alone *pre*dict, violent behavior." The literature on psychological tests published in the subsequent decade would do little to modify his conclusion.

McGuire (1976), in the most successful study predicting violent behavior with psychological tests, was able to equal Kozol et al.'s (1972) one-in-three accuracy rate in a controlled prison setting. She used a large variety of computer-combined test data (e.g., MMPI, Q-sort) to arrive at her findings. While noting that "the results do not justify the use of this approach to individual prediction in clinical settings" (p. 95), she observed that the computer analysis of relatively easily obtained test scores was considerably more economical than the intensive clinical approach. Whether her findings would obtain in the open community setting is not known.

CRITICISMS OF THE CLINICAL RESEARCH

The three major criticisms of the internal validity or logic of the clinical prediction studies reported to date are (1) that they are not really testing the accuracy of prediction, but rather something else, such as bureaucratic inertia or the effects of mental health treatment; (2) that it is not a fair test of predictive accuracy to measure violent behavior after a prolonged period of preventive institutionalization; and (3) that many of the people who show up in the research as "falso positives" are actually committing violent behavior but have not yet been discovered.

THE STUDIES TESTED SOMETHING OTHER THAN PREDICTION

It is sometimes claimed regarding the *Baxstrom* and *Dixon* patients that no one really believed that they would be violent if released—that the predictions were merely a bureaucratic ploy to keep "chronic" patients in the hospital—and so the finding that they were are not violent upon release should not be surprising. "In fact, the behavior of released patients may say more about institutional inertia than about poor predictions" (Stone 1975, p. 31).

It is difficult to respond to the criticism that mental health professionals were not telling the truth when they predicted violence so that they could facilitate their bureaucratic hold on patients. It may, unfortunately, be true that if the ticket to involuntary treatment is a prediction of violence, many psychiatrists and psychologists are willing to punch it (Monahan and Cummings 1975), regardless of whether they actually believe the patient to be violence-prone. The organizational contingencies operating upon mental health professionals to keep patients who are believed to "need" treatment, whether violent or not, may be intense.

Yet all research can do is take psychiatrists and psychologists at their word when they predict violence and assume the predictions are made in good faith. It is not an acceptable retort to the research for psychiatrists and psychologists to say, after the fact, that they did not *really* believe the patients to be violent. If bureaucratic pressure influences prediction, then that pressure is part of the social reality that should be empirically studied. And even in the case of the Baxstrom patients, *somebody* believed them to be violent, or else judo-training would not have been given to the staff of the civil hospitals to which they were sent (Rappaport 1973).

THE PREDICTIONS THAT WERE TESTED WERE SERIOUSLY OUT OF DATE

Alternatively, it is sometimes claimed that it is not fair to test a prediction of violence that is "stale" by several months or several years. It may be that the psychiatrists or psychologists were quite accurate in predicting that the patient was violence-prone *at the time of institutionalization.* But it is unfair to test this prediction after a person has had months or years of psychotherapy or medication or is simply that much older than he or she was at the time the prediction was made. Of course many people will not be violent. In fact, the argument goes, one would hope that none would be violent. This would mean that the treatment was completely effective.

A straightforward answer can be given to the criticism that the research is not fairly testing the prediction that led to the original institutionalization: the research is not testing these predictions at all. It is more properly viewed as testing the *final* predictions that were made before the patient or offender was released, usually by the courts.

Thus, the fact that the *Baxstrom* and *Dixon* patients were largely nonviolent when released from the hospital does *not* mean that the predictions that originally sent them there were wrong. It is impossible to tell one way or the other since too much happened before the original prediction was tested (treatment may have occurred and aging certainly occurred). What the research does show is that *the predictions that kept the patient in the hospital* were in error, since in 80 to 86 percent of the cases no violence was observed when the predictions were overruled by the Supreme Court. So the research is suspect only if taken as a test of the predictions that led to the original hospitalization. It appears valid if taken as a test of the final prediction made before release.

MUCH VIOLENCE MAY HAVE OCCURRED BUT NOT BEEN DETECTED

The strongest criticism of the existing prediction research is that it severely underestimates the extent of violent behavior committed by the individuals predicted to be violent, and thus many of those claimed to be "false positives" are actually "true positives" who have not yet been caught. To the extent this argument is valid, it seriously undercuts the thrust of the research findings.

There is no question that *some* underestimations of violence occurred in the research. The question is how much, so that a correction factor can be applied to the data obtained. Let us consider the problem in detail.

Each of the clinical prediction studies relied primarily upon *arrest* for a violent crime as its criterion measure. The Steadman studies included institutional assault and civil commitment for dangerousness along with arrest, and Thornberry and Jacoby (1979) also included civil commitment based on a dangerous act. How accurate an estimate of *violent behavior* is arrest for a violent crime, even if augmented by these other measures?

According to the National Victimization Panel (Department of Justice 1978)—a national study in which an interviewer inquires as to whether a citizen has been the victim of a crime in the past year—only 47 percent of the people who stated that they had been the victim of a violent crime reported the act to the police. In other words, 53 percent of the violent crime reported to the interviewer was not reported to the police. For several reasons, however, this dramatic figure appears somewhat inflated. Citizens who said they had not reported their victimization were asked the reason for not reporting. Twenty percent said that the act was "not serious enough" to report. Three percent said that it was "too inconvenient" to fill out a police form. Nineteen percent gave no classifiable reason for not reporting. As Levine (1976) has noted, "many trivial grievances which stay out of police records because people are not very upset are elevated to criminal status by the aggressive probing and searching of interviewers. . . . Since survey findings seem to include many of these trivial occurrences, the results are highly skewed and give an unrealistically grim portrayal of the crime problem" (p. 317). If one discounts those violent "crimes" that victims themselves believe are trivial, a reasonable estimate might be that of every three violent crimes committed in the United States two are reported to the police (cf. Levine 1976).

What of the violent crime that does get reported? The most recent FBI statistics (Webster 1978) reveal that the proportion of reported violent crime that is "cleared" by an arrest is approximately one-half (79 percent for murder; 52 percent for rape; 63 percent for aggravated assault; and 27 percent for robbery). One could conclude, therefore, that *of every three violent crimes that occur in the United States, two are reported to the police, and, of these, one results in an arrest.*

In terms of the criterion problem in prediction research, one could argue that since only one-third of the violent crime committed results in an arrest, it is hardly surprising that the "best" prediction studies can show only a one-third accuracy rate in predicting arrest. How could it be otherwise, since two-thirds of the criterion is hidden? Indeed, if one "corrected" for unreported and unsolved violent crime by multiplying the "true-positive" rate by a factor of 3, then instead of being only one-third accurate, the best prediction studies are in fact *perfectly accurate* in predicting arrest for violent behavior!

Several factors weigh heavily against such a large correction factor, however. The difficulty in the above argument lies in the assumption that violent behavior is evenly distributed among the population being predicted. If this were so—if, for example, each person predicted to be violent actually committed one violent act—then it would be true that a one-third accuracy rate in predicting arrest, which itself is only one-third accurate in estimating violent behavior, would in effect amount to virtually flawless prediction. There is much reason, however, to believe that violent behavior is far from evenly distributed.

Wolfgang (1978) interviewed a sample of the subjects in his Philadelphia cohort study. Offenders reported committing a mean of three "injury offenses" for each time they were arrested for an injury offense, with "recidivists" (those arrested between two and four times) reporting more than seven injury offenses per arrest. Likewise, the Rand study of habitual offenders (Petersilia, Greenwood, and Lavin 1977) found that offenders reported committing 10 felonies per arrest.

Indeed, if we accepted Wolfgang's figure of three violent acts per each arrest and used it to "correct" for the proportion of actual violence accounted for by those people who have been arrested for violent crime, we would conclude that *all* the violent behavior in the population is committed by those people who are eventually arrested for it.

Data such as those of Wolfgang and Petersilia would support the argument that *the one-third of the individuals predicted to be violent who are arrested for a violent crime are in fact the same people who are also committing most of the unreported and unsolved violent acts.* It is not that the "false positives" are really "true positives" in disguise, but rather that the "true positives" are in fact "truer" (i.e., more violent) than we have imagined. As Shinnar and Shinnar (1975, p. 597) have stated, "The important question is who commits the 70 percent of crimes which are never solved. . . . (T)he most likely possibility is that they are committed by the same group of recidivists who commit the 30 percent of crimes which are solved."

What, then, are we to make of the criticism that the use of arrest severly underestimates the number of people who commit violent acts and thus greatly inflates the number of "false positives?" Obviously, some of the unreported and unsolved violence is committed by persons who have escaped detection and are thus mislabeled as erroneous predictions. Obviously, too, some of the people who have been apprehended and thus validated the accuracy of a prediction have also committed more violence than has been ascribed to them. Pending future research and in light of the findings of Wolfgang (1978), Petersilia et al. (1977), and Shinnar and Shinnar (1977), I would offer the conclusion that current prediction studies provide *reasonably accurate estimates* of the validity of clinical predictions of violence, at least among populations of people who have high base rates for violence since they have committed it in the past. It should clearly be noted that this conclusion applies only to the kinds of situations studied in current research. It will be argued below that in some as-yet-untested situation, such as short-term emergency commitment, the validity of clinical prediction may be appreciably higher than has been reported. Likewise, clinical prediction with persons who do not have the history of violent behavior exhibited by the subjects studied in the current research would surely be less valid than the one-in-three ratios that have been reported.

To the extent that the current research does underestimate the occurrence of violent behavior, the overlooked behaviors are most likely those that are the least serious or that are directed against family members rather than against strangers (since family victims are least likely to report such acts to the police).

It should be noted that research has not yet addressed the issue of individual differences among mental health professionals regarding their ability to predict violence. It would certainly not be surprising if some were better than others at the task. In this regard, Shapiro (1977) studied the accuracy of physicians and medical students in predicting the occurrence of various rheumatic conditions. "In general," he found, "predictive skill was closely related to level of training. Faculty scored higher than residents, who in turn outscored students" (p. 1511). When actuarial tables were compared with clinical predictions, the tables were more accurate than the less experienced clinicians, and less accurate than the more experienced clinicians. Whether such findings would generalize from physicians predicting rheumatic disease to psychiatrists and psychologists predicting violent behavior is not yet known.

Shapiro (1977) also reported that the "error rate method" of evaluating the accuracy of clinical predictions (i.e., whether a prediction was ultimately right or wrong) was not nearly as sensitive in finding individual differences among physicians as was a mathematical "accuracy coefficient." The "error rate method" does not take into account the magnitude of the error (e.g., someone who predicts that an event has a zero probability of occurring is scored equally wrong as someone who predicts that the event has a 40 percent chance of occurring, if the event actually occurs), whereas the "accuracy coefficient" does. While "error rate" analyses could not distinguish among physicians in terms of their predictive success, "accuracy coefficients" revealed some physicians to be almost 10 times as accurate as others.

Finally, it should be recalled that the one-in-three accuracy rate discussed above is not "good" or "bad" in itself. Social values must be applied in order to evaluate the adequacy of this level of validity. Thus Gordon (1977) has written:

> [P]robabilities for individuals committing dangerous crimes within three years may seldom range higher than .3 to .5 in our society. When the probability becomes higher than that, it may apply to extremely unusual phenomena such as armed desperadoes on a killing rampage, or extremely trivial cases, such as bank robbers just before they leave their hideout on the way to a bank. In short, if we

inquired into the matter, we might find that probabilities that appear modest in absolute value actually describe the Babe Ruths of dangerousness, and that it is unrealistic to expect values ever to get any higher than that. When they do, the societal reaction may be to shoot first and ask questions later. What this means, then, is that if society is ever to protect itself routinely against individuals that it experiences as the most dangerous of all, it is going to have to do so at probability levels between .3 and .5 or not do it at all (p. 236).

POSSIBLE LIMITS ON THE GENERALIZABILITY OF THE RESEARCH: THE PREDICTION OF IMMINENT VIOLENCE IN EMERGENCY CONTEXTS

Claims that the studies inadequately tested mental health predictions or underestimated the criterion of violence are arguments against the "internal validity" of the research. Internal validity refers to the adequacy of the procedures used in the studies themselves, such as the degree to which any assumptions made were reasonable, the absence of logical flaws in the arguments made, and the appropriateness of the experimental design and statistical analyses for drawing the inferences desired. It was concluded that the existing research on violence prediction can withstand internal scrutiny reasonably well.

There is another kind of threat to validity that is frequently overlooked in debates about prediction research and that concerns "external validity" or the degree to which the conclusions of any research can be generalized to situations other than those directly studied (Campbell and Stanley 1966). If a study has poor internal validity, it must have poor external validity; it makes no sense to generalize a conclusion that is false on its own merits. But if a study has acceptable internal validity, as has been claimed for the research on the prediction of violence, it may still have poor external validity. One may not be able to generalize beyond the narrow facts studied.

Are there any reasonable limitations on the extent to which the conclusions of existing research—that no greater than one-out-of-three accuracy is possible—can be generalized? I believe that one situation may prove to be such an exception: prediction in short-term community contexts, such as emergency civil commitment and perhaps release on bail (Monahan 1978*b*).

While the major clinical and statistical (see chapter 4) studies of the prediction of violence differ from each other in many respects, most conform to the following methodological pattern:

1. Individuals were institutionalized. Institutionalization could have been on the basis of a criminal or juvenile arrest, conviction, or determination that an individual was a "mentally ill offender," "defective delinquent," or "incompetent to stand trial."
2. In the institution, predictions were made that a group of these individuals would be violent if released into the community. As previously mentioned, it was these predictions, made in the institution (jail, prison, or hospital), that were being tested in the research and *not* the predictions that may have occasioned the original institutionalization.
3. The group predicted to be violent was monitored for a number of years in the community on its actual performance of violent behavior. This was accomplished by checking police and (occasionally) mental health records.
4. Low frequencies of violent behavior were recorded, thereby revealing the inaccuracy of the predictions. Other studies compared groups predicted to be dangerous with those predicted not to be dangerous and found no differences.

What was tested in these studies? The most reasonable interpretation is that they tested predictions made in an institution of violence to occur in the open community. Persons who, for whatever reason, had been institutionalized for a substantial period of time (a mean of 15 years in the Baxstrom studies and not less than several months in any other study) were predicted to engage in violent behavior, if released into the open community. There were eventually released, and most were not violent.

While it is true that some studies included violence in the hospital as part of their criteria, the fact that "potentially violent" patients were likely to be medicated makes it unclear whether a lack of violence in the hospital reflected predictive inaccuracy or simply the pharmacological suppression of violent tendencies.

Rather than demonstrating that all forms of violence prediction are "doomed" as I have previously stated (Monahan 1976), a more discerning reading of the existing research suggests that it demonstrates the invalidity only of predictions made in one context that an individual will be violent in another, very different context. The context of prediction in the existing research is a closed institution in which the individual has resided for a significant period of time (several months to several decades). The context of validation is the open community.

There is an enormous body of research that would lead one to expect that the correlation between behavior predicted in one context and observed in another would be low (Mischel 1968, 1973; Bem and Allen 1974.) Since Hartshorne and May's finding in 1928 that the assessment of "moral character" was specific to the context in which it was measured, scores of investigations have reluctantly concluded that the cross-situational consistency of any type of behavior rarely exceeds the "sound barrier" (Arthur 1971) of a .40 correlation coefficient.

As Mischel noted, "Findings demonstrating the specificity of the interactions between persons and situations constrain how broadly we can generalize from an individual's behavior in any one situation to his reactions under different conditions. . . . Predictive validity tends to decrease as the gap increases between the behavior sampled on the prediction measure and the behavior that is being predicted" (1968, p. 323).

It is precisely this "gap" that exists in the current research on violence prediction. The jails, prisons, and mental hospitals in which predictions are made differ in obvious ways from the open community situations that are the truest test of predictive validity. This point is exacerbated by the fact that substantial time periods intervene between the point when the institutional prediction is made and the community validation is undertaken, and/or between the most recent exposure to the community context in which the prediction will be validated and the point at which the institutional prediction is made. In the former case, there is too much opportunity for the individual or the environment to change in unknown ways before the prediction is tested. In the latter case, the information on how the person behaves in the open community is made obsolete by the unknown changes that have occurred since he or she was institutionalized.

As Mischel noted, "The assessor who tries to predict the future without detailed information about the exact environmental conditions influencing the individual's criterion behavior may be more engaged in the process of hoping than of predicting" (1968, p. 140). It is the relative absence of current knowledge about the "exact environmental conditions" that are operating in the community context in which the individuals will be functioning which relegates long-term institutional predictions to the realm of whimsy.

To be sure, these are not the only reasons why violence has been inaccurately predicted under the circumstances investigated. However, they may help to account for the degree of inaccuracy that has been observed and may serve to differentiate the type of prediction that has been tested and found wanting from another type that has yet to be investigated, i.e., the prediction of imminent violence typically made in situations such as the short-term emergency commitment of the mentally ill.

In *emergency commitment*, a person residing in the open community is brought to the attention of a mental health professional, usually by a family member, friend, neighbor, or police officer, for a determination of whether he or she is mentally ill and a prediction of whether he or she will engage in violent behavior in the immediate future. A positive diagnosis and prediction result in the short-term "emergency" confinement of the person in a mental health facility.

Note the following differences between emergency commitment of this type and the kinds of prediction investigated in the research discussed earlier. In emergency commitment:

1. The context of prediction is the same as the context of validation. A prediction is being made in the open community that a person will

be violent in the same context. Often a prediction is made in a room in a home that the person will soon be violent in the same room.

2. The time between the point of prediction and the validation period is very short. Frequently the prediction is that the person will be violent in a matter of minutes or hours.
3. Since the prediction is being made in the same context in which it will be validated, there is little time intervening between the most recent exposure to the context of validation and the point of prediction. The prediction is made immediately after observing how the person behaves in the context in which the prediction would be validated. The information available to the predictor is thus fresh and current.

In emergency commitment, unlike the legal procedures studied in the current research, there is a small situational and temporal "gap" between the behavior used as a predictor and the outcome that is being predicted. One is directly sampling actions, e.g., threatening words and gestures, that are "as similar as possible to the behavior used on the criterion measures" (Mischel 1968), e.g., fulfilled threats. In violence as in other areas, it is potentially true that "predictions about individual behavior can be generated accurately from knowledge of the environments in which the behavior occurs" (p. 164).

Given the above factors, it would appear that there is a qualitative difference between predictions of violence made in the community for the purpose of short-term emergency commitment and those reported for longer term institutionalized patients and prisoners. Research on the failure to predict violence with more than one-third accuracy in the latter situation cannot reasonably be extrapolated to a similar conclusion in short-term emergency commitment cases. The prediction of violence, in this regard, may be analogous to the prediction of the weather: It is possible to predict poor weather with over 80 percent accuracy in the short run (i.e., 4 hours in advance), but predictive accuracy declines to about 30 percent over the longer term (i.e., 12 hours or more in advance) (Federal Aviation Agency 1965).

There are no data substantively relevant to the question of predictive accuracy in emergency commitment situations. The empirical question, therefore, is an open one. It is not capable of being resolved by recourse to the current existing body of research on violence prediction. There are theoretical considerations, discussed above, which suggest that predictions made under the conditions that typically apply in emergency situations *should* be better than those made in the institutional settings studied to date. But whether they are in fact better and, if so, how much better, is not now known. Unfortunately, for ethical and legal reasons (cf. Dix 1976; Monahan 1977), it is unlikely that direct research in situations that are defined as "emergencies" will be forthcoming.

SUMMARY

Research indicates that numerous childhood factors, particularly a history of early violence, relate to the commission of violent behavior as an adult. Outcome studies of clinical prediction with adult populations underscore the importance of past violence as a predictor of future violence, yet lead to the conclusion that psychiatrists and psychologists are accurate in no more than one out of three predictions of violent behavior over a several year period among institutionalized populations that had both committed violence in the past and were diagnosed as mentally ill.

Several criticisms have been made of the existing research on clinical prediction, among them that the studies tested something other than prediction, such as bureaucratic inertia, that the predictions were seriously out of date by the time they were tested, and that much violence may have occurred but escaped detection. Properly viewed, however, the research appears to weather these criticisms fairly well.

There does seem to be one major limitation that must be placed on the existing research on clinical prediction. That research took place in the context of long-term institution-to-community predictions. It may be that short-term "emergency" predictions in a person's normal environment generate more accurate estimates of violent behavior. These situations, in any event, have not yet been studied.

The next chapter considers how a mental health professional might go about maximizing the accuracy of clinical predictions of violent behavior.

Chapter 4

STATISTICAL APPROACHES TO IMPROVING CLINICAL PREDICTION

What steps can clinicians take to improve the accuracy of their predictions of violent behavior? At least two modifications of traditional clinical practice hold promise for augmenting predictive validity: an increased emphasis upon using statistical concepts in clinical prediction, and a heightened sensitivity to environmental or contextual variables. The former is considered in this chapter and the latter in the next. The goal in both cases will be to provide psychiatrists and psychologists with tools to incorporate in their clinical decisionmaking.

CLINICAL AND ACTUARIAL PREDICTION

THE NATURE OF THE DISTINCTION

Much has been made in the area of prediction of the distinction between "clinical" and "actuarial" (or "statistical") methods. In what is still the leading work on the subject, Meehl (1954) distinguished the two approaches as follows:

> The mechanical combining of information for classification purposes, and the resultant probability figure which is an empirically determined

> relative frequency, are the characteristics that define the actuarial or statistical type of prediction. Alternatively, we may proceed on what seems, at least, to be a very different path. On the basis of interview impressions, other data from the history and possibly psychometric information of the same type as in the first sort of prediction, we formulate, as in psychiatric staff conference, some psychological hypotheses regarding the structure and dynamics of this particular individual. . . . This type of procedure has been loosely called the clinical or case study method of prediction (p. 3-4).

Clinical and actuarial prediction may be thought of as differing along at least two dimensions, the *data* employed and *methods* used to turn the data into a prediction.

Actuarial tables spell out *precisely* what kinds of data are to be considered in the prediction, while the clinical approach appears to let the choice of data vary somewhat with the individual case. Thus in an actuarial table one would either *always* include or *never* include a factor such as birth order for specified types of cases, while clinicians might decide for whatever reason that birth order is relevant in one case but not in another case of the same general type. Also, there is a tendency in practice for clinicians to rely on—or, at least, to think they rely on—data at a *higher level of abstraction* than that typically used in actuarial prediction (e.g., "ego strength" rather than "age at first arrest").

In terms of the methods used to convert the data into a prediction, actuarial approaches use *automatic* or *mechanistic* decision rules that involve mathematical manipulation of the data (frequently no more complicated than adding up a total score), while clinical approaches tend to rely more upon an *intuitive* or subjective combination of the factors deemed relevant (Elstein 1976).

In practice, clinical and actuarial approaches function very differently. Yet it is important to keep in mind that they are merely *ends of continua* regarding the collection of data and methods for transforming the data into predictions. Almost all data have some subjective element to them ("Was he *really* the first-born?"; "Do step-brothers count?"), and there are identifiable commonalities in "intuitive" clinical decision rules.

A clinician who simply memorized an actuarial table and applied it rigorously in every case would obviously produce the exact same results as the table, even though he or she would be using "clinical judgment" in choosing that particular table in the first place. Likewise, actuarial tables can be constructed that rely entirely on data that must be obtained through clinical judgment (e.g., "add ego strength score to impulse control score and subtract maternal deprivation score," etc.).

It may be useful to distinguish the *data* and the *methods* of prediction as separate factors altogether (cf. Meehl 1954, p. 18). This would result in four "pure" kinds of prediction:

1. *Statistical data combined statistically* (e.g., age, sex, etc., in an actuarial table). Insurance company life-expectancy tables operate in this manner.
2. *Statistical data combined clinically* (e.g., a psychologist gives a prediction after looking at psychological test scores).
3. *Clinical data combined statistically* (e.g., probabilities of violence are attached to given psychiatric diagnoses).
4. *Clinical data combined clinically* (e.g., persons in certain diagnostic categories are assumed to react violently when their manhood is threatened). Many psychodynamic predictions function in this manner.

Again, most prediction in practice mixes these four types, particularly with regard to the data employed. Most clinicians no doubt take into account statistical data such as the patient's sex and age, along with clinical findings regarding diagnosis. Some actuarial tables include clinical diagnosis and demographic indices.

In virtually all of the studies that have tried to compare clinicians and actuarial tables in predicting the same events, the tables have proven the more accurate (Meehl 1954; Sawyer 1966). Indeed, so many studies have reached this conclusion that "actuarial prediction is better than clinical prediction" has become a truism in psychology. It should be noted, however, that not all accept this reading of the research. With regard to the quality of the studies upon which the actuarial-is-better conclusion rests, Holt (1978, p. 12) has stated, "No matter how impressively high it is piled, garbage remains garbage." One problem Holt sees with the studies is that most of them were designed by statisticians who have a vested interest in the outcome of the debate.

> Thus, the statistician takes advantage of the foolish boast of the clinician, "Anything you can do, I can do better," and plans the contest on his own grounds. The clinician ends up trying to predict grade-point average in the freshman year by a "clinical synthesis" of high school grades and an intelligence test. This is a manifest absurdity: under the circumstances, how could the clinician do other than operate like a second-rate computer? If clinical judgment is really to be tested, it must operate on data that are capable of yielding insights. Moreover, it hardly makes any more sense to expect it to grind out numerical averages of course grades than to expect an actuarial table to interpret dreams (Holt 1978, p. 27).

ON PREDICTING AN INDIVIDUAL'S BEHAVIOR FROM CLASS MEMBERSHIP

A philosophical problem frequently arises in actuarial prediction concerning the legitimacy of inferring statements about an *individual case* from the fact that a person belongs to a certain *class of cases* that have *X* probability of violence.

In truth, all one can say in actuarial prediction is that the person whose behavior is being predicted has characteristics X, Y, Z, and that *other* persons who have been studied in the *past,* who have had characteristics X, Y, and Z, have committed violent acts at a certain rate.

This issue applies equally to clinical prediction insofar as one makes the inference that, for example, because in a psychiatrist's previous experience those paranoid schizophrenics whose masculinity has been threatened have been violent, *this* threatened paranoid schizophrenic patient will also be violent.

Allport, a leader of the clinical (what he calls "ideographic") approach to assessment, has stated:

> Where this [actuarial] reasoning seriously trips is in prediction applied to the single case instead of to a population of cases. A fatal

nonsequitur occurs in the reasoning that if 80 percent of the delinquents who come from broken homes are recidivists, then *this* delinquent from a broken home has an 80 percent chance of becoming a recidivist. The truth of the matter is that *this* delinquent has either 100 percent certainty of becoming a repeater or 100 percent certainty of going straight. If all the causes in his case were known, we could predict for him perfectly (barring environmental accidents). His chances are determined by the pattern of his life and not by the frequencies found in the population at large. Indeed, psychological causation is always personal and never actuarial (cited in Meehl 1954, p. 20).

Meehl (1954, p. 20) agrees with the philosophical thrust of Allport's statement but notes that *"if nothing is rationally inferable from membership in a class, no empirical prediction is ever possible"* (italics in original).

There is, in Allport's paragraph, a subtle implication that by non-actuarial methods you can predict "for sure." It is interesting to note that in spite of his dislike for actuarial concepts he begins the crucial sentence with "His chances are determined." The whole notion of someone's "chances" is, as Sarbin has emphasized, an implicitly actuarial notion (p. 20).

What is necessary to make the inferential leap from membership in a class that has in the past been violent to the prediction that this member of the same class will in the future be violent is a *theory* linking the conditions operating to produce violence in the past class of cases with the conditions operating to produce violence in this specific present case.

As Underwood (1979) has recently written:

The importance of a causal theory is not that it guarantees the continuing effectiveness of the predictive scheme, but that it suggests the circumstances under which the scheme will remain effective. A statistical correlation in data about one group of people may not hold when used as a basis for predictions for another group of people. A causal theory helps to identify any relevant differences between the two groups, or differences in the surrounding circum-

> stances. Changes in the job market could remove a previously valid connection between lack of education and parole failure; changes in the typical employment patterns of men and women may remove the connection between male gender and short life (p. 1446).

An analogy may be instructive. If asked to predict in which direction this monograph would fall, if it were let go, the reader could technically state only that every other solid object he or she has let go in the past has (eventually) fallen down rather than risen up or remained suspended. What allows for the prediction that *this* object, if released in the future, will also fall down is that we possess a theory—gravity—that can plausibly let us generalize from the past class of cases to the current individual case. This theory also allows us to set boundary conditions on the prediction, so we know that, if the monograph were let go in space, outside the force of the earth's gravity, it would not fall but would remain stationary.

The catch, of course, is that we understand gravity much better than we understand violence and tend simply to assume that whatever conditions operated to produce violence in the past will also do so in the future. This may often be a plausible assumption, but there are exceptions, particularly if the time or situational gap between those persons studied in the past and the person to be predicted in the future is great. The violent crime rate among those under 18, for example, has increased by about 300 percent since 1960 (Wolfgang 1978). Therefore, more weight should now be given to "under 18" as a predictor of violence than should have been given in 1960.

As Gottfredson et al. (1978, p. 54) have put it:

> [U]sing an actuarial parole aid is a little like using a weather report that says there will be a 60 percent chance of rain. What the weather report actually means is that on similar days it has rained 60 percent of the time. It does not tell whether or not it will actually rain today. Nevertheless, such information can be useful in deciding whether or not to carry an umbrella.

ACTUARIAL STUDIES OF THE PREDICTION OF VIOLENCE

Wenk, Robison, and Smith (1972) reported three massive studies on the prediction of violence undertaken in the California Department of Corrections. The first study, begun in 1965, attempted to develop a "violence prediction scale" to aid in parole decisionmaking. The predictor items employed included commitment offense, number of prior commitments, opiate use, and length of imprisonment. When validated against discovered acts of actual violence by parolees, the scale was able to identify a small class of offenders (less than 3 percent of the total) of whom 14 percent could be expected to be violent. The probability of violence for this class was nearly three times greater than that for parolees in general, only 5 percent of whom, by the same criteria, could be expected to be violent. However, 86 percent of those identified as potentially violent, were not, in fact, discovered to have committed a violent act while on parole.

The second study reported by Wenk et al. (1972) was undertaken in 1968, also in regard to parole decisionmaking. On the basis of actual offender histories and psychiatric reports, 7,712 parolees were assigned to various categories keyed to their potential aggressiveness. One in five parolees was assigned to a "potentially aggressive" category and the rest to a "less aggressive" category. During a 1-year follow-up, however, the rate of conviction and imprisonment for crimes involving actual violence for the potentially aggressive group was only 3.1 per thousand (5/1630), compared with 2.8 per thousand (17/6,082) among the less aggressive group. Thus, for every correct identification of a potentially aggressive individual, there were 326 incorrect ones.

The final study reported by Wenk et al. (1972) sampled 4,146 California Youth Authority wards. Attention was directed to the record of violence in the youth's past, and an extensive background investigation was conducted, including

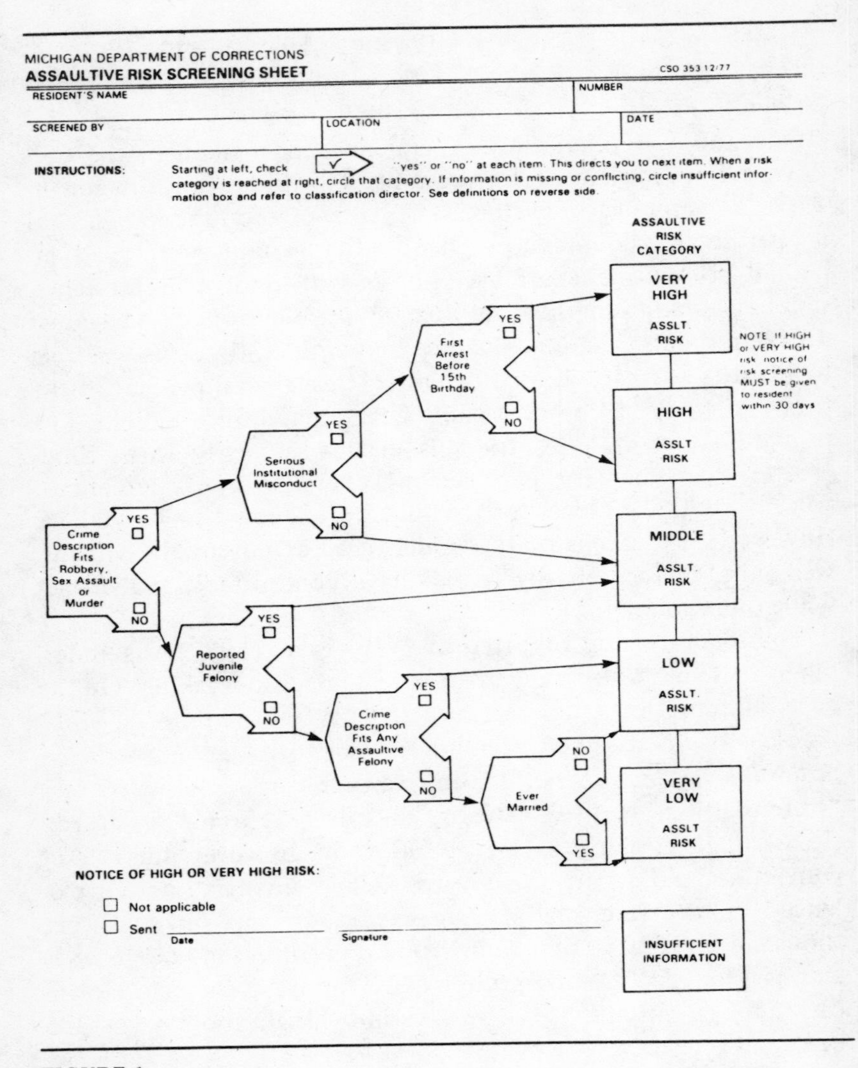
MICHIGAN DEPARTMENT OF CORRECTIONS

ASSAULTIVE RISK SCREENING SHEET CSO 353 12/77

RESIDENT'S NAME | NUMBER

SCREENED BY | LOCATION | DATE

INSTRUCTIONS: Starting at left, check ✓ "yes" or "no" at each item. This directs you to next item. When a risk category is reached at right, circle that category. If information is missing or conflicting, circle insufficient information box and refer to classification director. See definitions on reverse side.

NOTICE OF HIGH OR VERY HIGH RISK:

☐ Not applicable

☐ Sent ____________ Date ____________ Signature

INSUFFICIENT INFORMATION

FIGURE 1

psychiatric diagnoses and a psychological test battery. Subjects were followed for 15 months after release, and data on 100 variables were analyzed retrospectively to see which items predicted a violent act of recidivism. The authors concluded that the parole decisionmaker who used a history of actual violence as his sole predictor of future violence would have 19 false

TABLE 4 Violent recidivism rate of Michigan assalutive risk categories

Risk category	*Recidivism rate**	*Percent of sample*
Very high risk	40.0%	4.7%
High risk	20.7	6.6
Middle risk	11.8	45.5
Low risk	6.3	23.5
Very low risk	2.0	19.7

*Base rate for recidivism = 10.5 percent.

positives in every 20 predictions, and yet "there is no other form of simple classification available thus far that would enable him to improve on this level of efficiency" (p. 399). Several multivariate regression equations were developed from the data, but none was even hypothetically capable of doing better than attaining an eight-to-one false positive to true positive ratio.

The Department of Corrections of the State of Michigan (1978) has recently implemented an actuarial prediction device, the Assaultive Risk Screening Sheet, for use in program assignment and parole decisionmaking. Data on 350 variables were collected for 2,200 male inmates released on parole in 1971. Statistical analyses were performed on the data for half the subjects to derive an actuarial table relating to arrest for a new violent crime while on parole. The follow-up period was a mean of 14 months. The resulting factors were then applied to the other half of the subjects to validate the predictive accuracy of the scale. The scale is presented in figure 1, and the results of the validation study are in table 4.

Note that 40-percent accuracy on the basis of simply checking off the type of crime committed, the nature of institutional behavior, and whether an arrest occurred before the inmate's 15th birthday provides a higher degree of predictability than most of the clinical studies have been able to achieve after months of extensive (and expensive) examinations. Note, too, that such a degree of predictability applied to less than 5 percent of the sample.

As to why the Michigan study produced results so superior to the California studies, several factors are involved. Wenk et al.

(1972) reported base rates of violent behavior of 5 percent, 2.5 percent, and 0.3 percent in their three studies. This compares with a base rate for violence of 10.5 percent in the Michigan research–between 2 and 35 times higher than the California base rates. Part of these differences may be accounted for by variations in the meticulousness with which the recidivism data were collected. But the major reason accounting for the largest difference in base rates is that Wenk et al. (1972, Study 2) used *convicted and returned to prison* as their criterion, whereas the Michigan researchers used *arrest* for a violent crime as their index of violence. Since a large number of factors having nothing to do with violent behavior affect arrested individuals who are convicted and sent to prison (e.g., plea bargaining, prison overcrowding), the Michigan study may have the more accurate estimates of actual violence committed, despite the fact that the use of arrest overestimates violence to the extent that some, but few, innocent persons are included (Heumann 1978).

The Michigan Department of Corrections (Murphy 1980) has recently replicated their 1978 study using a sample of 1200 inmates released in 1974. The mean length of parole was 14 months, and the base rate for violent crime was 16%. The recidivism rates were only slightly less dramatic than the original study: 8.9% (very low), 11.1% (low), 17.4% (middle), 27.9% (high), and 32.0% (very high).

MAJOR ACTUARIAL CORRELATES OF VIOLENT BEHAVIOR

What factors have most consistently been related to violence in the research?

PAST CRIME, PARTICULARLY VIOLENT CRIME

If there is one finding that overshadows all others in the area of prediction, it is that the probability of future crime increases with each prior criminal act.

Following his cohort of Philadelphia males until they were 30, Wolfgang (1978) found that, if a person is arrested four times, the probability that it will happen a fifth is 80 percent. If a person is arrested 10 times, the probability of an eleventh arrest is 90 percent and the probability that the offense will be a serious or "index" offense (although not necessarily a violent one) is 42 percent. The PROMIS Research Project in Washington, D.C., analyzing arrest data on over 45,000 criminal defendants, found that the probability of rearrest for a person with five or more prior arrests "began to approach certainty" (Shah 1978*a*). Steadman et al. (1978) found that virtually all the violent crime committed by released mental patients is committed by patients who had an extensive criminal record *before* going into the mental hospital.

Further, the amount of crime attributable to repeat or chronic offenders, as mentioned previously, appears to be a substantial portion of the crime committed in society. Fifty-three percent of all crime committed by Wolfgang's (1978) birth cohort was committed by the 6 percent of juveniles who had five or more arrests. By the time they were 30, this group of chronic offenders had risen from 6 percent to 15 percent of the sample.

The 49 habitual offenders in the Rand study (Petersilia et al. 1977) reported committing over 10,000 crimes. Over a 20-year criminal career, they averaged 20 serious crimes per year of "street time" (i.e., time not spent in jail), with two of those crimes being violent ones. They admitted to committing 10 felonies for each time they were arrested. The PROMIS Research Project (1977) in Washington, D.C., likewise found that persons with a record of previous violent crime committed a disproportionate amount of violence. This study also found a significant degree of nonspecialization among offenders: "Today's petty larceny defendant may have been involved in a past robbery case and might be the subject of a future homicide prosecution or simple assault arrest" (p. 13).

AGE

At the extremes, the relationship between age and crimes of violence is self-evident. Infants do not mug, nor do geriatric patients rape. It is the precise configuration of the inverted

U-shaped relationship between age and crime that is at issue, and it clearly varies by the type of crime and by many other factors. The general thrust of recent research, however, is that the curve is strongly skewed toward the young and is becoming even more skewed.

In 1975, males between 15 and 20 years of age represented 8.5 percent of the American population and 35 percent of the arrests for violent crimes (Zimring 1978). Juvenile violence appears to be increasing more than twice as fast as that of adults, almost tripling between 1960 and 1975 (Wolfgang 1978). Not only one's current age, but the age at which one first comes in contact with the police, appears to relate strongly to criminal behavior. The Philadelphia cohort study (Wolfgang et al., 1972) found that the probability of being an adult offender was three and one-half times greater if one had been a juvenile offender than if one had not.

The average age at which the habitual offenders in the Rand study (Petersilia et al. 1977) committed their first serious offense was 14, with first arrest following a year later. The parole guidelines used in Michigan (1978) distinguish between *high* risk for assaultive recidivism and a *very* high risk for such conduct solely on the basis of whether one was *arrested* for any crime before his 15th birthday. The violent recidivism rate for Michigan parolees with an arrest record by the time they were 15 was 40 percent, almost double the 21 percent violent recidivism rate for those without such an arrest.

As violence feeds on the energy of youth, so age mellows even the most habitual offender. The Rand study found that habitual offenders committed an average of 3.2 serious crimes per month as juveniles, 1.5 per month as young adults, and 0.6 as adults. William Butler Yeats had said it earlier, "The years have put water in my blood and drowned the wildness within it."

Boland and Wilson (1978) concluded that "the best evidence now available suggests rather strongly that juveniles, especially chronic juvenile offenders, commit a far larger portion of serious crimes than arrest reports had previously led us to believe

[and] that the rate at which they commit these crimes declines as they get older. . . ."

It should be noted with regard to age, as it will be with race and economic status, that these findings refer only to "street" violence. The more subtle, but perhaps more harmful, forms of violence–manufacturing unsafe products, building lethal dams, and operating fatal coal mines–are among the less savory habits of the middle-aged.

SEX

Approximately 9 of every 10 persons arrested for a violent crime in the United States in 1977 were male (Webster 1978), and this ratio has been amazingly consistent since such statistics were first recorded. While there has been a substantial increase in female violent crime in recent years, it has been matched by an equally substantial increase in male violent crime. Granted that there are clearly sex biases in police arrest policies regarding some forms of crime (e.g., prostitution), it is highly unlikely that the police are systematically discounting the female perpetrators of murder, robbery, and aggravated assault. While police statistics do understate violence occurring in the home, it is unknown whether the violence of mothers against their children is more prevalent than the violence of husbands against their wives.

Hindelang (1976), reporting on a victimization survey of 78,000 people in eight major American cities, found that the victims of assault perceived their offenders to be female in 4 percent of the cases involving theft and in 12 percent of the cases not involving theft. Female victims reported their assailant to be female more often than did male victims (20 percent versus 5 percent for assault without theft). Hindelang concludes that "both male and female victims are disproportionately victimized by offenders who are perceived to be male and that offenders who are perceived to be female disproportionately choose females for victims" (p. 178).

Since most of the recent research on the habitually violent offender has focused on males alone, it is difficult to analyze patterns of female criminality.

Maccoby and Jacklin's (1974) definitive review of sex-linked behavior found that the fact that males are more aggressive than females to be one of the few sex differences to be well established by empirical research.

> The sex difference in aggression has been observed in all cultures in which the relevant behavior has been observed. Boys are more aggressive both physically as well as verbally. They show the attenuated forms of aggression (mock-fighting, aggressive fantasies), as well as the direct forms more frequently than girls. The sex differences are found as early as social play begins–at age 2 or 2-1/2 (p. 352).

A review of laboratory research on aggression by Frodi, Macauley, and Thorne (1977) concluded that sex differences in aggression are not as prevalent as commonly believed and that women may be as aggressive as men under certain conditions, such as when the aggressive act is perceived as justified. The ecological conditions operating in the open community, however, appear to elicit sex parity in aggression relatively infrequently. Not only are the base rates of violent behavior in the general population significantly lower for females than for males, but the recidivism rate of female offenders is lower than that of male offenders (Kelley 1977).

RACE

"In the end," Silberman recently noted, "there is no escaping the question of race and crime" (1978, p. 117).

> To say this is to risk, almost to guarantee, giving offense; it is impossible to talk honestly about the role of race in American life without offending and angering both whites and blacks–and Hispanic browns and native American reds as well. The truth is too terrible on all sides; and we are all too accustomed to the soothing euphemisms and inflammatory rhetoric with which the subject is cloaked (p. 117-118).

Blacks accounted for slightly less than 12 percent of the American population in 1977 but accounted for 46 percent of all arrests for violent crime, varying from 39 percent of the arrests for assault to 57 percent of the arrests for robbery.

Perhaps the most distressing finding from the Philadelphia cohort study was the degree to which race affected the data. Blacks were four times more likely to have an arrest record than whites. When one weights the offenses for seriousness, the differences become even stronger. Wolfgang (1977) recently reported that "nonwhites in their sixteenth year inflict more social harm, through delinquency, on the community than do all whites from age 7 to 18. Nonwhites 7-10 years old have a weighted crime rate 11 times that of whites. At no age is the racial difference less than a factor of four."

Hindelang (1978) attempted to assess the extent to which black overrepresentation in arrest statistics reflects differential *involvement* by blacks in crime or differential *selection* of blacks for arrest by the police. He compared FBI arrest statistics for common-law, personal crimes with the racial identification of offenders made by victims to the National Victimization Panel. While finding some evidence of police bias, he concluded that the "data for rape, robbery and assault are generally consistent with official data on arrests and support the differential involvement hypothesis."

As further evidence in support of the differential involvement hypothesis for black overrepresentation in arrest statistics, Silverman (1978) reported that Puerto Rican New Yorkers, who are, as a group, poorer and less educated than black New Yorkers, have only one-third the arrest rate of blacks for violent crimes. Mexican Americans in south Texas have one-eighth the conviction rate of black Texans for robbery.

> It would be hard to convince a Puerto Rican New Yorker that the police treat Puerto Ricans more deferentially than they treat blacks. It would be even harder to persuade Mexican-Americans in the Southwest that they receive preferential treatment from the police (p. 120).

As Hindelang noted with respect to his data, however:

> These results cannot be extrapolated beyond the specific crimes to which the analyses were addressed. If the differential involvement in

white-collar offenses, organized crime, corporate crime, or consumer fraud had been studied the results might have been very different. Obviously these data and analysis shed no light on racial differences in crime generally (p. 107).

SOCIOECONOMIC STATUS AND EMPLOYMENT STABILITY

In a recent review of predictors of criminal recidivism, Pritchard (1977) reported that eight of the nine studies with relevant data found an offender's pre-prison income level to relate to performance on parole. Further, 72 of the 76 studies reporting data on the stability of pre-prison employment found a lack of stability to indicate failure on parole. In a recent Massachusetts study, Cook (1975) found that 89 percent of parolees who had a satisfactory job at the end of their first year on parole completed parole successfully, while only 50 percent of those not satisfactorily employed did so. The probability of recidivism during the second 3 months on parole increased directly with the number of jobs held during the first 3 months, from 11 percent recidivism when one job was held to 43 percent recidivism when five jobs were held.

In the Rand study, only 43 percent of the habitual offenders had a minimally acceptable job while on the streets as an adult (cf. Tittle, Villemez, and Smith 1978).

OPIATE OR ALCOHOL ABUSE

In Pritchard's (1977) review, all nine of the studies on pre-prison opiate abuse found it to relate positively to criminal recidivism.

Forty-three percent of the Rand sample were classified by the California Department of Corrections as addicted to or users of narcotics. Sixty percent of the Rand sample said they committed their crimes under the influence of alcohol, drugs, or both, and about half of those stated that this condition contributed to the commission of the crimes. Offenders involved with both alcohol and drugs committed more than twice the number of crimes against persons as did offenders involved with neither, although alcohol alone tended to have no effect in this study.

The desire for money to buy drugs and alcohol was cited by only 10 percent of the habitual offenders as the reason for their beginning a career of crime, but by about 33 percent as the reason for their continuing in crime.

A study recently done by Schmidt and Witte (1978) on several thousand persons released from North Carolina prisons concluded that the person at highest risk of returning to prison was a "young, black, male alcoholic with many previous convictions."

To be sure, there are other correlates of serious criminal recidivism. There has been an amazing turnaround in sociological attitudes toward the role of low IQ in influencing criminal behavior, with several recent studies finding that it does indeed have a substantial effect (Hirschi and Hindelang 1977). Residential mobility and marital status (State of Michigan 1978) also seem frequently to come through as factors distinguishing recidivists from one-timers. While there is clearly a large degree of overlap among the items listed (i.e., "common variance" is accounted for), each does appear to have some independent effect.

It should be noted, however, that the presence of one of these predictors may greatly reduce the relevance of another. Thus race, taken in isolation, bears a substantial relationship to violent crime. But the relevance of race *in a person with an extensive record of violence* appears minimal or nonexistent. Whatever their race, people with such records have a higher probability of future violent behavior. Such findings lead one "to emphasize the unimportance of race as a determinant [of future violence] once the individual has been identified as a delinquent" (Hamparian, Schuster, Dinitz, and Conrad 1978, p. 133).

For the purpose of clinical predictions made by mental health professionals, what is *not* listed as a major statistical correlate of violent behavior is at least as important as what is listed. The most relevant noncorrelate of violence is "mental illness."

MENTAL ILLNESS AND VIOLENT BEHAVIOR

Mental illness and violent behavior have always been linked in popular belief. Brydall, writing in 1700, traced the roots of civil commitment of the mentally ill in England to "the old Roman law" which provided that "Guards or Keepers be appointed for Madmen not only to look that they do not mischief to themselves, but also that they be not destructive to others. . . ." (quoted in Dershowitz 1974). After Daniel McNaughten was acquitted by reason of insanity in 1843, the *Times* of London published this ditty (quoted in Greenland 1978):

> Ye people of England exult and be glad
> For ye're now at the mercy of the merciless mad.

The first mental hospital in the American colonies was founded at the urging of Benjamin Franklin, who relied heavily on the argument that the mentally ill were prone to violence. In his petition to the Pennsylvania Assembly he set forth the claim (quoted in Monahan and Geis 1976):

> That with the Numbers of People, the Number of Persons distempered in Mind and deprived of their rational Faculties, has greatly increased in this province; That some of them going at large are a terror to their neighbours, who are daily apprehensive of the Violences they may commit.

Likewise, in the mind of the modern public, the correlation between violence and mental illness remains, due in no small part to a systematic exaggeration by the media of the crime rates of the mentally ill (Steadman and Cocozza 1978).

There is a growing and converging body of empirical research on the relationship between violence and mental illness. It addresses two questions: (1) What is the prevalence of psychiatric disorder among prison populations? and (2) What is the violent crime rate of people released from mental hospitals? While answers to these questions will not provide an entirely satisfactory account of the relationship between violent behavior and mental disorder, since a large portion of diagnosably disordered persons have never been in mental hospitals and a large portion of violent offenders successfully avoid prison, they do provide a useful antidote to popular mythology.

MENTAL ILLNESS AMONG CRIMINALS

Bolton (1976) reported the results of a psychiatric epidemiological survey of inmates of adult jails and juvenile detention facilities in five California counties. Over 1,000 adult offenders and 650 juveniles were examined. He reported that 6.7 percent of the adults and 2.9 percent of the juveniles were diagnosed as psychotic; 9.3 percent of the adults and 20.6 percent of the juveniles were found to have a nonpsychotic mental disorder. "Personality disorders" were reported for 21.0 percent of the adults and 25.2 percent of the juveniles. Monahan, Caldeira, and Friedlander (1979) found that police officers estimate that 30 percent of the persons they arrest are at least "somewhat" mentally ill, but only 12 percent are either "moderately" or "severely" mentally ill. Roth and Ervin (1971, p. 429) concluded that "psychiatric morbidity in criminal populations is probably somewhere between 15 and 20 percent."

Considering that the President's Commission on Mental Health (1978, p. 8) recently concluded that "as many as 25 percent of the population are estimated to suffer . . . emotional disorders at any time," and given that the social classes from which "street" offenders are drawn are disproportionately represented in that figure, the findings of Bolton (1976), Monahan et al. (in press), and Roth and Ervin (1971) do not indicate an increased rate of mental illness among jail inmates.

Clearly the most comprehensive study of rates of psychiatric disorder among offender populations has been performed by Guze (1976). Guze's review of the literature is representative of the conclusions of others (e.g., Brodsky 1973).

> Overall, the other studies may be summarized as follows. Psychosis, schizophrenia, primary affective disorders, and the various neurotic disorders are seen in only a minority of identified criminals. There is no complete agreement as to whether any of these conditions is more common among criminals than the general population, but it is clear that these disorders carry only a *slightly* increased risk of criminality if any at all (Guze, pp. 35-36; italics in original).

Guze's own study of 223 male and 66 female felons in Missouri arrived at the following findings:

> Sociopathy, alcoholism, and drug dependence are the psychiatric disorders characteristically associated with serious crime. Schizophrenia, primary affective disorders, anxiety neurosis, obsessional neurosis, phobic neurosis, and brain syndromes are not. Sexual deviations, defined as illegal *per se,* are not, in the absence of accompanying sociopathy, alcoholism, and drug dependence, associated with other serious crime.

Diamond (1974), commenting on Guze's earlier work, notes that sociopathy, alcoholism, and drug dependence "are precisely those psychiatric states which are less easily definable and less generally agreed to be illnesses at all" (p. 448). Indeed, Guze defined "sociopathy" for the purposes of his research as follows:

> This diagnosis was made if at least two of the following five manifestations were present in addition to a history of police trouble (other than traffic offenses): a history of excessive fighting . . . school delinquency . . . a poor job record . . . (and) a period of wanderlust or being a runaway. . . . For women, a history of prostitution could be substituted for one of the five manifestations (p. 35).

If all prostitutes who have ever been truant in school, or all unemployed males with a period of "wanderlust" in their history are counted as "sociopaths," it is not difficult to understand why 78 percent of all male and 65 percent of all female felons were so diagnosed.

With the exception of a higher prevalence of the "disorders" of alcoholism and drug dependence, therefore, prisoners do not appear to have higher rates of diagnosable mental illness than their class-matched peers in the open community.

VIOLENT BEHAVIOR AMONG FORMER MENTAL PATIENTS

An interesting pattern exists in the data on violent crime rates of former mental patients. Almost without exception, studies performed in the 1950s and earlier found that released patients had a *lower* rate of arrest for violent behavior than the general population (Ashley 1922; Pollock 1938; Cohen and Freeman 1945; Brill and Malzberg 1954), while studies performed in the 1960s and 1970s have consistently found a *higher* rate of violent behavior among former patients than among the nonpatient population (Rappaport and Lassen 1965; Giovanni and Gurel 1967; Zitrin, Hardesty, Burdock, and Drosaman 1976; Durbin, Pasewark, and Albers 1977; Sosowsky 1978). What accounts for this wholesale shift in the research findings?

According to Cocozza, Melick, and Steadman (1978; see also Steadman, Cocozza, and Melick 1978), the apparently increased crime rate among former patients reflects "the changing clientele of state hospitals." They examined the arrest records of almost 4,000 patients released from New York State mental hospitals in 1968 and 1975 using a 19-month follow-up period. Particular attention was paid to whether or not the former patient had ever been arrested *prior* to being sent to the hospital. Since their findings for both years were similar, only the 1975 data are presented in table 5.

A striking pattern of results emerges. While it is true that former patients, as a group, do have a substantially higher arrest record for all types of crime than does the general population, patients without an arrest record *prior* to going to the hospital have a *lower* arrest rate than the general population. Patients with *one* arrest prior to going to the hospital have a slightly higher than average arrest rate for violent crime once they get out of the hospital (except for sex crimes which are substantially higher). Patients with *two or more* prior arrests have a

TABLE 5 Annual arrest rates per 1,000 for felonies for the general population, total patient sample, and patients with zero, one and two or more prior arrests—1975 sample*

	General population	*Total patient sample*	*Patients with no prior arrest*	*Patients with one prior arrest*	*Patients with two or more prior arrest*
	(N=12,320,540)	(N=1,938)	(N=1,428)	(N=187)	(N=323)
Total arrests	32.51	98.50	22.06	138.00	413.50
Arrests for violent crimes	3.62	12.03	2.21	3.37	60.46
Arrests for potentially violent crimes	2.83	6.18	0.88	3.37	31.21
Arrests for sex crimes	0.45	2.60	0.44	6.74	9.75

*From Cocozza, Melick, and Steadman, 1978

drastically higher violent crime rate than the general population. *Thus, compared with the general population, the higher rate of violent crime committed by released mental patients can be accounted for entirely by those patients with a record, particularly an extensive record, of criminal activity that predated their hospitalization.* This is consistent with the literature on violent crime among criminal populations: A record of past violence is the best predictor of future violence.

But why the *increase* in violent crime rates among released patients in recent years? Steadman, Cocozza, and Melick (1978) compared their findings with those reported by Brill and Malzberg (1954) on a comparable population of New York patients released in 1947. The results of the two studies are almost identical except that *only 15 percent of the 1947 patients had a prior arrest record while 40 percent of the 1975 subjects did.* As Brill and Malzberg noted 25 years ago:

> Arrests in the ex-mental hospital patients were largely concentrated in a relatively small, rather well-demarcated group of persons with a previous criminal record, and their anti-social behavior was clearly

> correlated with well-known factors which operate in the general population and was not correlated with the factors of mental illness except in a negative way . . . [An] attack of mental illness with hospitalization does not tend to leave an inclination toward criminal activity greater than that which existed prior to the illness and . . . does not produce such a tendency if it did not previously exist . . . (pp. 12-13).

Rabkin (1979 p. 25) came to a similar conclusion in her exhaustive review of every study published on the topic:

> At the present time there is no evidence that [released patients'] mental status as such raises their arrest risk; rather, antisocial behavior and mentally ill behavior apparently co-exist, particularly among young, unmarried, unskilled poor males, especially those belonging to ethnic minorities.

The real issue, therefore, is not what psychological factors account for the increased crime rate among released mental patients, but rather what sociological and economic factors underlie the administrative and political decision to send more criminals to mental hospitals in the first place. As chronic-geriatric patients—who have a very low crime rate—are being "deinstitutionalized" from mental hospitals into nursing homes, the proportion of beds that are being filled by younger and more violent persons—who in the past might have been sent to jail or prison (Stone 1975)—is rising. As Steadman et al. (1978, p. 820) have noted, "If one were to gather a group of men of whom 40 percent had previously been arrested, from the general population, it is quite likely that the arrest rates found among the 1975 former patient group would be duplicated or exceeded."

In terms of specific psychiatric diagnoses, the New York study found a significant association between patients diagnosed as drug or alcohol abusers or "personality disorders" and future criminal behavior. While no more than 8 percent of any other diagnostic category was subsequently arrested, 18 percent of patients with alcohol or other drug-related diagnoses were arrested as were 28 percent of those diagnosed as "personality disorder" (Steadman, Cocozza, and Melick 1978). With the substitution of "sociopathy" for "personality disorder," these are the same three factors identified in Guze's (1976) study of mental illness in a prison population. As was the case with sociopathy, it is unclear what "personality disorder" means in this context and how independent it is from a history of past criminal behavior.

As stated by the President's Commission on Mental Health (1978, p. 56), "The sporadic violence of so-called 'mentally ill killers' as depicted in stories and dramas is more a device of fiction than a fact of life. Patients with serious psychological disorders are more likely to be withdrawn, apathetic, and fearful. We do not deny that some mentally ill people are violent, but the image of the mentally ill person as essentially a violent person is erroneous."

THE DOMINANCE OF CLINICAL PREDICTION IN THE LAW

If actuarial or statistical prediction has advantages over the clinical approach in terms of precision, reproducibility, or efficiency, why has clinical prediction dominated in the legal system? Kastermeier and Eglit (1973) offered several reasons to account for the primacy of the clinical approach: (a) the view that legal decisions are intrinsically individualized; (b) the fact that actuarial prediction explicitly acknowledges that errors will be made (and therefore decisionmakers may feel more responsible for the mistakes, even though they may be fewer than a clinical approach would produce); and (c) the view (see below) that some important case-specific factors will not be considered in statistical formulae. Carroll (1980) added two other reasons, "(d) uneasiness over stating some reasons for decisions that are not part of the statistical predictions (e.g., public opinion, personal impressions, and private attitudes), and (e) concern over loss of status or even loss of job in competition with statistical formulae." One final reason for preferring clinical to actuarial approaches might be called (f) uneasiness over stating some reasons for decisions that *are* part of the statistical predictions (e.g., the inclusion of such socially sensitive variables as race and sex in prediction equations). It is for this reason that clinical prediction sometimes functions as a "laundering" of actuarial prediction by hiding the nature of the variables used in the prediction from public view (see chapter 1).

The above six reasons for preferring clinical to actuarial prediction are primarily of a negative sort. They refer to weaknesses in the legal system or in human decisionmakers that lead them to prefer one method over the other. Are there any *good* reasons for preferring clinical to actuarial prediction? At least three possibilities arise.

CLINICAL PREDICTION AND THE RARE EVENT

It is true that some important case-specific factors may be overlooked in the actuarial approach (reason (c) above). Meehl (1954) gives the example of predicting whether "Professor A" will attend the movies on a given night. Presume that an actuarial table has been developed that predicts with a probability of .90 that the professor will attend the movies. The clinician, however, knows that, in addition to fulfilling all the criteria in the table for a .90 probability, the professor has just broken his leg. "This single fact is sufficient to change the probability of .90 to a probability of approximately zero" (p. 25). Note that one could not incorporate such rare contingencies as breaking a leg into the actuarial table, since, precisely because they are rare, they would not appear as statistically significant in a large prediction study.

> In other words, such a factor does not appear as statistically important in the mass event, but if the clinician knows the fact in the case of Professor A, he (correctly) allows it to override all other data in the Table. . . . [T]hese rare cases furnish one of the respects in which the human brain can be a very sensitive indicator (Meehl 1954, p. 25).

So there may indeed be some case-specific factors that could allow a human being to make a more accurate prediction than an actuarial table in a given individual case. Some formal prediction schemes such as the one used by the U.S. Parole Board allow for just such a "clinical override," when the persons responsible for the prediction believe that the results of an actuarial table are inaccurate in a given case (Gottfredson, Wilkins, and Hoffman 1978). Yet elsewhere Meehl (1973, p. 85) cautions that "clinicians should beware of overdoing the broken leg analogy."

> There are at least four aspects of the broken leg case which are very different from the usual "psychodynamic" reversal of an actuarial prediction. First, a broken leg is a pretty objective fact, determinable with high accuracy, if you care to take the trouble; second, its correlation with relative immobilization is near perfect . . . ; third, interaction effects are conspicuously lacking–the immobilization phenomenon cuts neatly across the other categories under study; fourth, the prediction is mediated without use of any doubtful theory. . . . (p. 85).

It may be, Meehl states, that clinical prediction as a whole is less accurate than actuarial prediction, but that for a subset of cases for which clinicians express high confidence in their predictions, the clinicians are more accurate. "Once having proved this, we could thereafter countermand the formula in cases where the clinician expresses high confidence in his head" (1973, p. 89). We should note, however, that such proof has not yet been reported (see Shapiro 1977).

INSUFFICIENT TIME FOR ACTUARIAL ANALYSIS

A second reason for preferring clinical to actuarial predictions of violence is that situations may arise in which time does not exist to permit a review of the individual's record and his or her scores on the other variables that may be included in an actuarial table. It is difficult to imagine, for example, how much actuarial information could be collected in the context of an emergency 72-hour civil commitment evaluation. While one could judge a person's sex, and estimate age and intoxication status, many other potentially relevant variables could be ascertained only from external sources that are not available in the context of the "emergency" situation. At least until more complete actuarial information can be compiled, "intuitive" clinical judgment (taking into account, e.g., the vehemence of shouted threats) may be the only feasible short-term prediction strategy (Meehl 1973, p. 170).

THE UNAVAILABILITY OF ACTUARIAL DATA

In addition, as argued previously, there exists little actuarial knowledge concerning what variables predict violence in short-term "emergency" situations. We do not know what to look for, even if we had the time to find it. In situations where no actuarial data exist, reliance upon clinical expertise is the only approach available, if decisions are to be made on predictive grounds. Meehl (1973, p. 89), in this regard, asks rhetorically whether professionals will use clinical or actuarial techniques in making predictive decisions. He answers: "Mostly we will use our heads, because there just isn't any formula. . . ." " 'Clinical experience' and 'common sense,' " he notes, "must be invoked when there is nothing better to be had" (p. 59).

THE CLINICAL USE OF STATISTICAL DATA

Perhaps too much has been made in the past of distinguishing actuarial and clinical methods and not enough of how each might contribute to the other. From the beginning, clinical methods have been pitted against actuarial ones in the academic equivalent of a cockfight. Recall that the title of Meehl's 1954 book was "Clinical *Versus* Statistical Prediction." The tone of much of the actuarial writing (except for Meehl himself, 1973) was not chosen to win psychiatric friends or influence psychological colleagues.

> To the practitioner, dealing every day with life-and-death decisions, the message of much of the [actuarial] work is, "Your judgment is

> not nearly as good as you think it is," which is a threat to the security, self-esteem, and even the professional identity of many clinicians. Small wonder that they find it easy to ignore work that lies largely outside their field, seems of dubious relevance, and is clearly still embroiled in controversy (Holt 1978, p. 16).

Yet clinical prediction, as noted, may take into account actuarial tables, and actuarial prediction may incorporate clinical judgments. One possible strategy for improving clinical prediction, therefore, suggests itself. It is to provide clinicians with as much actuarial information as possible, to see if this affects their predictions.

On the first point, Hoffman et al. (1974) presented actuarial prediction tables to parole board members reviewing the files of adult male inmates for parole consideration. The board members were then asked for their own clinical predictions and for a decision on whether the inmates should be paroled or kept in prison. They found that the correlation between statistical risk estimates based on the actuarial tables and the board's clinical risk estimates was 0.74 when the actuarial tables were presented to board members before they made their clinical judgments and 0.53 when the tables were not provided. The correlation between risk estimates and the outcome of the parole decision was 0.30 when the actuarial tables were provided and 0.18 when they were not. The provision of actuarial data, therefore, affected both the clinical judgments of the parole board and its parole decisions in the predicted direction.

A complicating fact is that Hoffman et al. (1974) also found that actuarial data were more likely to result in increased clinical predictions of unfavorable parole outcome (when the actuarial data suggested such an unfavorable outcome) than they were to result in increased predictions of favorable outcome (when the actuarial data were in the favorable direction). This could mean even more false positives.

The reason that actuarial estimates indicating violent behavior may have more of an effect upon clinical prediction than actuarial estimates indicating nonviolence may involve the social consequences of each type of error for the clinician doing the predicting. If one overpredicts violence, the result is that individuals who will not be violent are institutionalized. This situation is not one likely to have significant public ramifications for the individual responsible for the overprediction. But consider the consequences for the predictor of violence should he or she in the other direction–underprediction. The correctional official or mental health professional who predicts that a given individual will not commit a dangerous act is subject to severe unpleasantness should that act actually occur. Often he or she will be informed of its occurrence in the headlines ("Freed Mental Patient Murders Mother") and will spend many subsequent days fielding reporters' questions about professional incompetence and institutional laxity. As Steadman (1972) noted, "There may be no surer way for the forensic psychiatrist to lose power than to have a released mental patient charged with a serious crime in the district of a key legislator." Given the drastically different consequences of overprediction (or "type 1 errors") and underprediction (or "type 2 errors") for the individual responsible for making the judgment, it is not surprising that he or she should choose to "play it safe" and err on the conservative side. Note that if the clinician adopted the strategy of simply providing estimates of the likelihood of future violence and left it to others in the legal system (e.g., judges) to decide whether the likelihood exceeds the threshold necessary for taking preventive action, these potentially biasing social contingencies might be attenuated (see chapger 1).

In practice, therefore, if *either* clinical *or* actuarial estimates indicate violence, the prediction is likely to be that violence will occur, while it may take both actuarial and clinical estimates of safety to result in a prediction of nonviolence.

How, then, is the clinician to improve the accuracy of his or her prediction by taking statistical data into account? Several steps appear advisable:

(1) Making Base Rates of Violence a Prime Consideration

If the base rate of violent behavior in a given population is very low, prediction becomes an extremely difficult task. As

Megargee (1976, p. 18) has it, "(m)ental health professionals should limit themselves to predicting dangerous behavior in high base-rate populations such as those who have already engaged in repeated violence."

It should be noted that the "population" for which a base rate is estimated should be as specific and relevant as possible (Meehl 1973, p. 38). The base rate of violent behavior for a person brought to a mental health center by the police as potentially "dangerous to others" is *not* the base rate of violence in the general population, or even the age- and sex-adjusted base rate of violence in the general population. It is *the rate of violent acts committed by other people who have been referred by the police as dangerous.* This base rate (which to my knowledge is not available and therefore would have to be estimated) may be very different from that of the general population.

Carroll (1979), in a series of ingenious studies, examined what factors influence whether decisionmakers take base-rate information into account in making predictive decisions. Subjects in several parole prediction studies were more likely to make use of statistical data when these data were explicitly associated *with the individual case* whose behavior was being predicted rather than in terms of group rates (see the discussion of predicting from class membership earlier in the chapter). As Carroll 1980 notes:

> Subjects . . . were presented with the information that a group of parolees had a known recidivism rate, and that each case they examined was drawn from this group. They apparently failed to complete the syllogism by saying "therefore, each case has an expected risk of recidivism equal to that of the group. . . ."
>
> Clearly then, the reasoning process is difficult and not immediately obvious to subjects. The completion of this reasoning process . . . by simply assigning a risk level to the individual case, does result in use of the risk information. . . . These results are consistent with very recent work showing that base-rate information will be used if a *causal connection* is apparent between the characteristics about which the base-rates are given and the events to be predicted (Tversky and Kahnemann, in press).

In addition to giving predictions in individual rather than group form, Carroll (1980) also found that statistical information that was stated in *verbal* form was more influential in affecting clinical judgment than statistical information stated in *numerical* form. If subjects were told that "the computer" revealed that a person had a "good" parole prognosis, they were more influenced than if told that the computer concluded the person had a "75 percent" chance of parole success. Indeed, when presented with numerical risk statements of 35 percent, 55 percent, and 75 percent chance of parole success, the subjects' clinical predictions distinguished between 35 percent and the latter two values, but did not distinguish between 55 and 75 percent success. That is, as Hoffman et al. (1974) found, statistical information was used to increase one's prediction in an *unfavorable* direction, but it was ignored when it indicated a favorable outcome. When the statistical data were translated for the subjects into verbal terms such as "good" or "poor" risk, however, subjects did distinguish between a favorable and a neutral prediction. Thus, "a set of verbal categories in which to present statistical risk predictions appears to be the most effective presentational mode currently available" (Carroll 1980).

(2) Obtaining Information on Valid Predictive Relationships

Clearly, the clinician is better off with no statistical information than with erroneous information. One purpose of this monograph is to disseminate the results of recent research on factors predictive of violent behavior. Yet, in an area as rapidly developing as this one, "continuing education," particularly self-education, is a clear necessity. Clinicians need to be alert and sensitive to illusory correlations. Given the tendency for such correlations to persist, continuing education and inservice training programs need to emphasize such sources of error in clinical judgments.

Also, more information does not necessarily lead to better predictions. In fact, a surplus of information may reduce predictive accuracy. Bartlett and Green (1966) studied the ability of psychologists to predict student grades. In one condition, psychologists were given four pieces of information (e.g., high school rank), and in another they were given the same four items plus 18 additional ones (e.g., father's education). In every case, the psychologists predicted more accurately with fewer items of data. Disturbingly, however, they were more confident of their predictions the more data they had available to them.

Focusing on a limited number of *relevant* and *valid* predictor items, therefore, is more important than an exhaustive examination that yields much irrelevant and ultimately confusing information.

(3) Not Overreacting to Positive Associations

There is little that can be said here other than to exhort my fellow clinicians not to overreact to one positive index of violence at the expense of overlooking several negative indices, as we appear prone to do.

A *balanced* search for information on factors that would decrease an individual's propensity for violent behavior (e.g., strong family support), as well as factors that would increase violence proneness, should be undertaken. In addition, it should be noted that simply because a pattern of positive and negative evidence appears to be highly "representative" of future violent behavior does not mean that such behavior should be predicted to occur (Kahneman and Tversky 1973). The base rate and the reliability of the available evidence must also be considered.

> For example, if only 10% of a particular group are expected to engage in future violent behavior on the basis of prior probabilities (base rates), and if the specific evidence concerning the predictions is of poor reliability (e.g., clinical assessments and certain psychological test indices), then the predictions should remain very close to the base rates. The greater the move away from the base rates under the above conditions, the greater will be the probability of error (Shah 1978*a*, p. 229).

SUMMARY

One of the most promising avenues for improving the accuracy of clinical predictions of violent behavior appears to be an increased emphasis upon incorporating statistical concepts into clinical decisionmaking.

Statistical prediction differs from clinical prediction both in the kinds of data it employs and in the methods it uses to convert the data into a prediction. Statistical prediction uses lower order, often demographic, variables and combines them by means of automatic, mathematical rules. Clinical prediction, by contrast, is less precise about the predictor variables used and may choose different predictors for different cases. These factors are then transformed into a prediction in a subjective or intuitive way.

The research studies on the statistical prediction of violent behavior have yielded a wide variety of results, ranging from substantially less accurate to substantially more accurate than the studies of clinical prediction, depending upon what criterion of violence was used. The factors most closely related to the occurrence of violent behavior appear to be past violence, age, sex, race, socioeconomic status, and opiate or alcohol abuse. Estimated IQ, residential mobility, and marital status also are related to violent behavior. Mental illness, however, does not appear to be related to violence in the absence of a history of violent behavior. When one controls for demographic variables, prisoners do not appear to have a higher incidence of mental illness than the general population. Mental patients who do not have a record of violent arrests are, if anything, less violent than the general population.

Despite the advantages of statistical prediction, the clinical approach may be superior when dealing with rare events that were not anticipated in statistical analyses. It is also true that for many situations, particularly short-term "emergency" ones, no statistical information has yet been developed.

The clinician who wishes to improve the accuracy of his or her predictions by incorporating statistical information can best do so by making the base rates of violent behavior a prime consideration, obtaining data on factors that actually relate to future violence, and not overreacting to a positive indicator of violence at the expense of overlooking several negative ones.

Chapter 5

ENVIRONMENTAL APPROACHES TO IMPROVING CLINICAL PREDICTION

We have already noted the importance of considering contextual or environmental factors in predicting violence and the fact that some experienced clinicians have recognized this importance for some time.

The use of environmental or situational variables in prediction differs from the use of personal or dispositional variables in at least one major way. In the case of dispositional variables, one has only to establish a relationship between the predictors and the criterion. Since the dispositional variables refer to fixed or relatively enduring characteristics of the person, one knows immediately whether any obtained relationship can be applied to a given case: An individual subject will not change from white to black, from male to female, or from 45- to 25-years-old over the duration of the follow-up. With situational predictors, however, one must establish *both* a statistical relationship between a given situation and violent behavior, and the probability that the individual will, in fact, encounter that situation. One might, for example, predict with a high degree of accuracy that a given class of offenders will resort to violent behavior when confronted with a situation they interpret as a challenge to their masculinity. To predict the actual occurrence of violent behavior, one would then have to perform a separate prediction concerning whether they will encounter such a situation during the period under investigation.

It can be argued that the inclusion of situational variables is the most pressing current need in the field of violence prediction. The principal factor inhibiting the development of situational predictors of violence is the lack of comprehensive ecological theories relating to the occurrence of violent behavior.

ASSESSING ENVIRONMENTAL FACTORS

Moos (1973) has identified six different ways of conceptualizing human environments which have been used in previous research:

1. *Ecological dimensions,* including meteorological, geographic and architectural variables
2. *Dimensions of organization structure,* including staffing ratios and organization size
3. *Personal characteristics of mileu inhabitants,* implying that the character of an environment depends upon the characteristics (e.g., age, sex, abilities) of those who inhabit it
4. *Behavior settings,* defined by Barker (1968) as units with both behavioral and environmental components (e.g., a basketball game)
5. *Functional or reinforcement properties of environments,* suggesting that people vary their behavior from one setting to another principally as a function of the reinforcement consequences in the different environments
6. *Psychosocial characteristics and organizational climate,* in which the characteristics of an environment as perceived by its members are measured on various psychosocial scales

Of these six conceptualizations of human environments, two (ecological dimensions and dimensions of organizational structure) appear not to be relevant to the prediction of individual violence—although a hot summer day does increase the probability of an urban riot, and architectural modifications have much potential for preventing violence (Heller and Monahan 1977)—and another (behavior settings) is in an insufficient state of development to allow for its current application to the topic of prediction. The remaining three provide guidance for the formation of environmental predictors of violence.

Conceptualizing environments in terms of the personal characteristics of milieu inhabitants might lead a mental health professional to inquire of a person whose behavior is being predicted with whom he or she is living, working, and interacting socially. The pooled base-rate probabilities of violence for these individuals (given their age, sex, and prior history of violence, for example) should, according to this approach, relate significantly to the probability of violent behavior being committed by the individual.

Emphasizing functional or reinforcement properties would lead to a behavioral analysis of the reward contingencies operating in the environments in which the predicted individual would be functioning. If, in a given environment, desired rewards (e.g., material goods, peer approval, self-esteem) can be obtained only by committing violent behavior, then the probability of violence in this environment would be high.

Finally, environments may be conceptualized for the purpose of prediction according to their psychosocial characteristics and organizational climate. According to Moos, the "social climate" perspective "assumes that environments have unique 'personalities' just like people. Personality tests assess personality traits or needs and provide information about the characteristic ways in which people behave. Social environments can be similarly portrayed with a great deal of accuracy and detail" (1975, p. 4). He devised a series of scales to measure the perceived social climates of prisons, hospital wards, community-based treatment programs, classrooms, military units, and families. Common to all these scales are three basic dimensions of the environment: (a) *relationship dimensions,* such as the degree to which the environment is supportive and involving; (b) *personal development dimensions,* such as the degree of autonomy the environment provides; and (c) *system maintenance and system change dimensions*, including the degree to which the environment emphasizes order, organization, and control.

It should always be clear that these methods of describing environments overlap greatly and that some situational predictor items would fit equally well under any of the rubrics. It should also be clear that situational variables are being proposed for use in addition to, rather than instead of, dispositional variables in clinical prediction schemes. It is the *interaction* of dispositional and situational variables that holds the greatest promise for improved predictive accuracy. Ideally, it eventually might be possible to make differential predictions of the sort that individuals with dispositional characteristics of type N would have X probability of violent behavior, if they resided in environment type A, and Y probability if they resided in environment type B. But to reach this nirvana of prediction, it is necessary for researchers to begin the arduous task of compiling and verifying a catalog of situations that relate to the future occurrence of violent behavior. What follows is a very preliminary attempt to do that.

MAJOR SITUATIONAL CORRELATES OF VIOLENT BEHAVIOR

Despite its early stage of development, much may be learned from the study of environments in terms of predicting individual violence. The following are what appear to be the best candidates for situational or environmental correlates of violent behavior that potentially can be of use for prediction in the individual case. The first three can be conceptualized either as environmental "support systems" used by an individual for coping with life stress (President's Commission on Mental Health 1978), or as the sources of the life stress itself (see chapter 5).

FAMILY ENVIRONMENT

One of the best predictors of whether released mental patients will survive in the community without being rehospitalized is the degree of support provided by their families (Fairweather, Sauders, and Tornatzky 1974). As Stone (1975, p. 13) stated, "a principal social function of the law-mental health system is to provide technical care for those individuals who are temporarily or permanently extruded from society's principal caretaking unit, the family. The wisdom and morality of this extrusion and the quality of this technical care are the bedrock problems of the law-mental health system."

In the case of violent behavior, the family context is crucial since family members are so frequently the victims of violent behavior (Monahan, 1977*b*). Skodol and Karasu (1978), as noted previously, found that, in 77 percent of emergency commitment cases in which the patients admitted to actively considering violence, the victims were family members. The frequency of violence in police family-crisis interventions has been well documented (Bard 1969; Driscoll, Meyer and Schanie 1973).

The family environment may be critical because of its role in supporting or discouraging violent behavior on the part of the family member whose behavior is being predicted. The probability of a person being violent may be greater if he or she resides in a family that encourages robbery as a career and where violence by other family members is a frequent occurrence, than if he or she has support and models for nonviolent modes of interaction and needs satisfaction. Though their prior records may be the same, the probability of recidivism of a released offender living with grandparents on a farm may be substantially less than that of another offender living with alcoholic friends in an inner city.

PEER ENVIRONMENT

There is an enormous sociological literature on "peer group influences" on behavior, particularly adolescent behavior. Likewise, numerous psychological studies attest to the effects of one's friends as behavior models (Bandura 1969). There is, in addition, ample folk wisdom about the effects of "getting in with the wrong crowd" on criminal activity. Gang violence is probably the paradigmatic case of peer-induced harm. To the extent that a person's violent behavior in the past has occurred in a particular social context (rather than "as a loner," for example), it may be important to ascertain whether the same peers who encouraged previous violence are likely to provide similar encouragement in the future. The person returning to the same friends who participated in the last robbery may have a greater likelihood of future violent crimes than the person who has broken contact with a criminally oriented support group.

JOB ENVIRONMENT

There is a growing body of research on the effect of employment upon criminal behavior, although the research generally does not separate violent from nonviolent crime (Monahan and Monahan 1977). At monthly intervals, Glaser (1964) interviewed a sample of 135 parolees released from Federal institutions in 1959 and 1960. In comparing the job-holding activity of the men who completed parole with that of men returned to prison, he found that the eventual successes acquired their first jobs sooner, and during the initial period of parole, earned a higher monthly income than did the eventual recidivists.

Cook (1975), studying 327 male felons released from Massachusetts prisons in 1959, found that 65 percent of those who held a "satisfactory" job (defined as a job which lasted 1 month or more) during the first 3 months of parole were eventually successful in completing an 18-month parole period compared with a 36 percent success rate among those who did not have a satisfactory job during the first 3 months. Seventy-five percent of parolees holding a satisfactory job during the second 3 months of parole were eventual successes, compared with 40 percent of those who did not hold a satisfactory job. Eighty-nine percent of those having a satisfactory job at the end of their first year on parole completed the parole period without revocation, while only 50 percent of those not satisfactorily employed successfully completed their term of parole.

Cook (1975) also found that steady job holding was related to parole success, while frequent job changing increased the likelihood that a parolee would recidivate. The probability of recidivism during the second 3 months on parole increased directly with the number of jobs held during the first 3 months, from 11 percent recidivism when one job was held to 43 percent when five jobs were held.

While such data do not prove a causal relationship between employment and crime (since some third factor may cause both the reduction in recidivism *and* whether one is employed), it would appear that holding a job that is both satisfying and supportive reduces the probability of recidivism for at least some criminal offenders.

AVAILABILITY OF VICTIMS

Violence, as Toch (1969) has emphasized, may be thought of as an interactional concept. It takes two for a murder to occur. Clearly, some persons are relatively indiscriminate in the victims they choose. Mergargee (1976, p. 8) quotes a steel worker interviewed by Studs Terkel in *Working:* "All day long I wanted to tell my foreman to go fuck himself, but I can't. So I find a guy in a tavern. To tell him that. And he tells me too . . . He's punching me and I'm punching him, because we actually want to punch somebody else" (Terkel, 1974, p. xxxiii). Consistent with the frustration-aggression hypothesis and theories of displacement, it is likely that both parties to this dispute would have found other "victims" had they not chanced upon each other.

There may be other types of individuals who are quite specific in their choice of victim and will not be violent other than to a given victim or class of victims. Spouse murderers, for example, have a very low recidivism rate since they have removed their source of irritation. Incest offenders may desist when their children grow up. The now famous *Tarasoff* case (1976) is a clear example of victim-specific violence (Roth and Meisel 1977; Wexler 1979). A client revealed in therapy his intention to kill a woman who had rejected his romantic interests. The client then committed no violent acts for 2 months while the woman was on vacation. Shortly after she returned home, he murdered her. As Shah (1978*b*) has noted:

> Decision-makers may wish to know whether the dangerous acts are more likely to occur against some *particular persons* (e.g., a spouse or girl friend, the individual's own children, or a neighbor with whom longstanding conflicts have occurred); and/or against some *broader group* of people (e.g., minor boys or girls in the case of a pedophile, adult women in the case of certain exhibitionists or rapists, etc.); and/or a *more dispersed segment of the community* (e.g., the likely victims of "purse-snatchings" and other street robberies, potential victims of recidivistic drunken drivers, etc.) (p. 180).

AVAILABILITY OF WEAPONS

Finally, the presence of weapons has long been held to be a situational instigation to violent behavior (Berkowitz and LePage 1967). Equally importantly, weapons may influence not the occurrence but the *severity* and *lethality* of violent behavior (Newton and Zimring 1970; Zimring 1977). The difference between assault and murder frequently revolves around whether the offender had a knife or only a fist at his or her disposal. The difference between murder and attempted murder likewise is often determined by whether the offender has access to a gun or a knife.

Just as the possession of the "means" to commit suicide is a frequently used predictor of suicide (Beck, Resnick, and Lettieri 1974), so the person who reveals possession of a household arsenal may be more likely to harm another than the individual without such means of destruction.

AVAILABILITY OF ALCOHOL

The evidence linking the excessive use of alcohol to violent behavior was noted in the last chapter. There is a great deal of literature on criminology relating the high frequency of violent behavior in and near bars and taverns (e.g., Wolfgang 1958). At least for those persons whose previous violent behavior has been associated with a state of intoxication, the easy availability of alcohol and the presence of a support group which encourages its excessive use (drinking buddies) may constitute a high-risk context for the occurrence of violent behavior.

ASSESSING INTERACTIONS BETWEEN PERSONS AND THEIR ENVIRONMENTS

It may well be that the very definition of a "situation" is interdependent with an individual's personality (Bem and Allen 1974). A situation that one person perceives as a threat to his or her social status may be perceived by another as nonthreatening or even status enhancing. People often *choose* the situations they are in (e.g., going to a bar that one knows has a high frequency of fights), and situations often draw certain kinds of people to themselves (e.g., pawn shops sometimes draw people with stolen property). How, then, are we to describe a "situation" or a "context" for the purpose of prediction? One major proposal was recently made.

Bem and Funder (1978) demonstrated that situations can be described in terms of how different types of people are expected to behave in them. The probability that a particular person will behave in a given way in a certain situation is a function of the similarity between his or her characteristics and the characteristics of the people (called "Templates" by Bem and Funder) that typically frequent the situation. For example, assume that for a given community program for offenders, records reveal that the people in the program who have assaulted other participants tended to be characterized as "highly resentful of authority," "refusing group activities," and "addicted to heroin." If one wished to predict whether *this* potential referral to the program would be assaultive, one would want to see how closely he or she matched these three characteristics. If the characteristics of the potential referral did indeed match the characteristics of the kinds of people who have been found to be violent in that environment in the past, the probability of favorable outcome would be decreased. If the characteristics of the potential referral were very different from those of the people who had been violent in that environment, a more favorable prediction could be made.

Note how this "situation-centered" perspective differs from the "variable-centered" perspective just discussed. Rather than ask what characteristics of situations *in general* relate to violent behavior, Bem and Funder (1978) ask how this *particular situation* influences different types of people to act. One situation may elicit violence in a certain kind of person and helping behavior in another. The question in predicting the behavior of a *particular person* in that environment, then, becomes whether he or she has more of the characteristics of the violent or of the helping person. A second environment may elicit violence from a completely different type of person.

Describing situations in terms of how given types of people are expected to behave in them may have much utility for preventing violence by modifying environmental characteristics (Monahan and Catalano 1976). But, for the purpose of predicting the behavior of an individual across a variety of environments in the community, there may be a better approach. "Rather than describing a situation in terms of how a set of hypothetical ideal persons behave within it, we should now describe a person in terms of how he or she behaves in a set of hypothetical ideal situations" (Bem and Funder 1978). For example, one could give an individual a set of items describing properties of situations (e.g., "is unstructured," "is characterized by the presence of an authority figure") and ask the person to state the degree to which these properties typify the situations in which he or she behaves violently. (There is a formal technique, the Q-Sort [Block 1961], in which statements are sorted into nine categories, from the least characteristic to the most characteristic of what is being measured. It might have utility for the purpose being discussed here [Bem and Funder 1978]).

Alternatively, if the individual was unable or unwilling to do the rating, a clinician familiar with the case or the file could do it. One way to decide whether a given item describes the kind of environment in which the individual can be expected to be violent is to rate the kinds of environment in which the person has been violent in the past. Thus, if the individual had four previous assaults, and two of them were against males and two against females, one would rate an item "victims tend to be females" as neither characteristic nor uncharacteristic of the environments in which violence has occurred. If all four victims were females, the item would be rated highly characteristic, and if all four were males, the item would be rated highly uncharacteristic.

After one has obtained a profile of the kinds of situations in which the individual is expected to be (or, better yet, has in the past been) violent, it remains to categorize the environments in which he or she will likely be functioning during the period for which one is predicting. Often, much of this environment will be unknown, but many characteristics may be available. For example, if one highly salient aspect of the environments in which a person committed previous assaults was that his wife was present in them as the victim, but the wife has since divorced him and moved to a different city, it might be possible to affix a substantially lower probability of violence than if the wife was still at home. While many other aspects of the individual's environment may be unknown, the presence or absence of the wife may be available information.

The approach put forward by Bem and Funder (1978) to categorize people in terms of the environments that elicit given behaviors from them has potential not only for improving the prediction of violent behavior, but for generating differential predictions that may be useful in placement or treatment decisions. If a person tends to be violent in environments characterized by factors A, B, and C, and one is faced with the choice of recommending that he or she be placed in one environment which is characterized by A, B, and D or in another setting which is characterized by factors A, D, and E, one might wish to recommend the latter, since only one of its three principal characteristics is similar to those that trigger violence in the individual, while two of the three characteristics of the former setting are similar.

The Bem and Funder (1978) model, therefore, poses three questions:

1. What characteristics describe the situations in which the person reacts violently?
2. What characteristics describe the situations which the person will confront in the future?
3. How similar are the situations the person will confront in the future to those that have elicited violence in the past?

Much more work needs to be done to develop the Bem and Allen (1974) and Bem and Funder (1978) procedures into practical clinical tools. Creative clinical experimentation with different methods of environmental assessment may be of great help in that development.

SUMMARY

A second way in which the accuracy of clinical prediction may be improved is through increased attention to situational or environmental predictors of violence. A disturbance or deficit in a person's environmental support systems, particularly the family, peer, and job-support systems, may trigger violent coping mechanisms. The easy availability of victims, weapons, and alcohol in the environment also may heighten the probability of violence.

One novel method of assessing the effect of environmental variables upon violent behavior is to assess a person in terms of the characteristics of the environments in which he or she becomes violent. The clinician would then estimate the characteristics of the environments in which the person would be functioning in the future and note any resulting similarities.

The final chapter attempts to synthesize these factors and others into prescriptions of how a mental health professional might go about assessing an individual's potential for violence.

Chapter 6

THE CLINICAL EXAMINATION

This chapter attempts to summarize and synthesize the foregoing material in a manner that may prove helpful to a mental health professional conducting an assessment of violence potential. It does so by offering a series of questions for the clinician to consider as he or she struggles with making a prediction. Attention to these questions along the lines suggested in the commentary may provide a structure for reaching a defensible estimate of the probability of violent behavior occurring in the future.

It is not without trepidation that a "model" format for the clinical prediction of violence is proposed. It should be clear from what has gone before that relatively few factors have proven their predictive mettle as antecedent conditions to violent behavior. Most of what follows represents nothing more (or less) than the professional judgments of persons experienced at the task of prediction, as I have interpreted and amplified them. It is offered as a reasonable guide to performing a kind of assessment that increasingly is being sought from mental health professionals. It is not offered as a substitute for a careful reading of the clinical literature on prediction cited in previous chapters (particularly the American Psychiatric Association

1974; Cohen et al. 1978; Kozol et al. 1972; Kozol, 1975; Megargee 1976).

It will be assumed that this assessment is solely for the purpose of predicting violent behavior *and not for the purpose of diagnosing mental disorder.* As noted earlier, violent behavior is not typically associated with mental disorder. Should the question of mental disorder also be of interest (e.g., for the purpose of civil commitment), an additional (or combined) examination would be in order. Should the issue of violence arise in the course of ongoing treatment, many of the factors that are assayed here may already be known and need only to be made explicit. The procedures outlined here are necessarily idealized and could be superseded in the context of very imminent violence. One need not estimate the IQ of someone screaming "I'll kill you!" and needing to be physically restrained from so doing.

I would emphasize once again my belief that, wherever possible, psychiatrists and psychologists should limit their role to providing an estimate of the probability of future violent behavior, substantiating that estimate with clinical and statistical evidence, and leaving to legislators or judges the decision as to whether preventive action should be triggered. Such a stance is not "passing the buck" to evade responsibility for difficult clinical decisions. It is forcing those in government to accept responsibility for difficult political decisions dealing with competing claims for freedom and safety. In matters of law, the buck must be permitted to pass until it stops at the doorstep of the legislature and the judiciary. Cohen et al. (1978, p. 39) have put it well:

> It is a perilous, narrow path between the requirements of social order and the expression of individual freedom. To balance order and liberty properly is a sociopolitical, not a clinical, issue, and this must be done by society's courts and legislatures. The clinician should neither be given nor attempt to usurp society's right to determine the risks it is willing to take in resolving the conflict between safety and liberty.

QUESTIONS FOR THE CLINICIAN

IS IT A PREDICTION OF VIOLENT BEHAVIOR THAT IS BEING REQUESTED?

Shah (1978*a*) has enumerated 15 points in the legal process at which estimates of future harmful conduct are taken. The first question to ask oneself is whether any questions of prediction are being raised in a given case and, if so, for what legal purpose? Such a question may seem excessively basic. Yet Geller and Lister (1978), in a study of psychiatric reports written for the purpose of determining competence to stand trial and criminal responsibility, found that 55 percent of the reports offered a prediction of "dangerousness" *even though one was not requested by the court.* At the same time, 65 percent of the reports did *not* address the issue of competency, and 93 percent did *not* address the issue of responsibility, which were the issues in which the court was interested.

Psychologists and psychiatrists are not alone in their confusion regarding questions to address. Farmer's (1977) study of presentence assessments performed for Federal court judges found that, in over 95 percent of the referrals to psychologists and psychiatrists, "judges consistently fail to communicate their objectives and questions" to the examiner. Judges surveyed found it difficult to say *why* they were requesting a mental health examination.

> Their answers suggested general and frequently nebulous concerns rather than a desire to have specific questions answered. For example, some would say that they just wanted to know more about the person, but could not readily explain what new information they sought (Farmer 1977, p. 7).

It would appear that the first task of the mental health professional is to be clear about whether anyone is interested in having a prediction made and, if not, what it is that they are interested in and what information is being sought. This may require going back to the source of the referral and requesting clarification of the task.

AM I PROFESSIONALLY COMPETENT TO OFFER AN ESTIMATE OF THE PROBABILITY OF FUTURE VIOLENCE?

Once one knows what the question is, one must consider whether he or she is the person to answer it. Candid introspection should take place concerning one's knowledge and understanding of (a) the theoretical and methodological literature on prediction and assessment in general; (b) the clinical and research literature on the prediction of violent behavior; and (c) the relevant legal framework in which the prediction would be offered (e.g., a State commitment statute). This monograph has attempted to provide guidance in the first two of these areas.

This introspection may lead to the conclusion that no one is competent to make the kind of prediction being requested; that some mental health professionals are competent to do so, but that the questioner is not among them; or that the questioner does indeed possess relative professional competence to address the issue at hand.

In assessing one's competence at this form of assessment, one may also wish to ascertain whether one possesses the disposition necessary to "objectively" evaluate the facts at issue. In this regard, Fisher (1976) found that the higher psychiatrists and psychologists themselves scored on the Rokeach dogmatism scale, the more likely they were to predict dangerousness for a sample of clinical cases.

ARE ANY ISSUES OF PERSONAL OR PROFESSIONAL ETHICS INVOLVED IN THIS CASE?

It has been argued repeatedly that, to the greatest extent possible, the clinician should defer to the policymaker regarding questions of social and political value raised by violence prediction. These questions concern the definition of the violence one is predicting, the factors one takes into account in predicting it, the degree of predictive accuracy necessary for taking preventive action, and the nature of the preventive action to be taken. They are questions for the legislature, the judiciary, and, ultimately, the voting public.

Two issues prevent this principled abdication of a policy role from being absolute. The first is that circumstances may arise in which the personal moral values of the mental health professional so clash with the accepted legal codes of society that the mental health professional, to maintain his or her own ethical integrity, should decline to participate in prediction altogether. Depending on the moral values of the mental health professional, the prediction of violent behavior for the purpose of imposing the death penalty, or the inclusion of certain variables (e.g., race) in prediction equations, may be examples of circumstances in which a clinician could decline, on principle, to participate in offering a prediction. (An analogy would be the refusal of physicians to perform abortions when to perform them would violate the physician's moral beliefs.) Note that here one is *not* using science as a subterfuge for promulgating one's preferred moral or political beliefs, as would be the case if a clinician, believing an offender to have a high potential for violent behavior, testified otherwise in court in order to save the offender from execution. Rather, what is being advocated is a general presumption in favor of deferring policy questions to those whose formal role in a democratic society it is to answer them, with the mental health professional reserving the right to opt out of the process entirely if the results, or the process of arriving at them, would compromise his or her ethical integrity (see Loftus and Monahan, 1980).

The second qualification on an absolute abdication of a policy role by mental health professionals is that all too frequently policymakers have evaded their responsibility to provide a framework in which mental health professionals can operate. Thus, no State yet specifies the level of probability of violent behavior necessary to invoke civil commitment as "dangerous to others" (Monahan and Wexler 1978). In many cases, the mental health professional can keep the ball in the appropriate court by simply stating his or her judgment (e.g., "Due to the following factors, Mr. X has a 50 percent probability of committing assault within the next two weeks.") and letting the policymaker decide whether such a prediction is "high enough" to invoke legal constraints. In other situations, however, particularly "emergency" ones in which there is simply not enough time to force the policymaker's hand, the options for the mental health professional who concurs with the position being argued here reduce to walking out of such situations muttering "When you people decide what you want, let me know" or reluctantly trying to fashion a workable framework within which to offer predictions, knowing full well the pitfalls involved. The crucial issue here would be to be explicit about what rules one was adopting and to follow them consistenly. Thus, in a State in which the law simply held that a person could be committed if he or she was "dangerous to others," a mental health professional in a psychiatric emergency admitting room responsible for commitment could state in a letter to the local judge:

> Since I can find no guidance on how to interpret the statute and yet feel it necessary to take action in many cases, I shall adopt this interpretation: "dangerous to others" shall be taken to mean A, B, and C; the probability of such events occurring shall be taken to be D; and the time frame in question shall be taken to be E. If you believe any of these interpretations to be improper, please inform me and I shall modify my procedures accordingly.

While such a statement may fail to endear the clinician to the judge, it is one way of attenuating the problems created when policy decisions fall by default upon his or her shoulders.

There is one final issue of professional ethics that will arise in all cases in which a clinical examination is performed. That issue concerns what to inform the examinee regarding the nature of the examination. Should the individual be informed of the *reason* he or she is being examined (e.g., civil commitment, parole, etc.), the potential *consequences* of the examination (e.g., 2 weeks in a mental hospital, an extended period of imprisonment), or the *level of confidentiality* that applies to what the individual reveals (e.g., a complete report to the judge and opposing as well as defense counsel)? The answer to each question, I would argue, is "yes." It is yes, not for reasons of *legal duty* (although such duties have been proposed), but rather for reasons of *professional ethics.* As a recent Task Force of the American Psychological Association (1978, p. 1104) stated:

> One crucial point in addressing confidentiality, as in addressing other dilemmas of the psychologist's loyalty, is that all parties with a claim on the psychologist's loyalty be fully informed in advance of the existence of confidentiality, or lack of it, and of any circumstances that may trigger an exception to the agreed-upon priorities. The individual being evaluated . . . then has the option of deciding what information to reveal and what risks to confidentiality he or she wishes to bear.

The ethical standards of both the American Psychiatric Association and the American Psychological Association support such honesty in the interests of client welfare. Without this openness, individuals being interviewed only for the purpose of assessing their violence potential, for example, may mistakenly believe that they are in the process of receiving treatment for their psychic pains.

GIVEN MY ANSWERS TO THE ABOVE QUESTIONS, IS THIS CASE AN APPROPRIATE ONE IN WHICH TO OFFER A PREDICTION?

Should one conclude that a prediction is not actually being requested, that one is not professionally competent to offer predictive judgments, or that one's ethical beliefs preclude rendering a prediction in this type of case, it is both appropriate and essential to decline to offer a professional opinion in the matter and to return the referral to its source with an explanation for the action taken.

Should the issue of violence prediction arise in the course of treatment and should the mental health professional lack confidence in his or her own abilities in this area, prompt consultation with a more knowledgeable colleague may be necessary.

Assuming that the case is one in which a prediction is appropriate, the following questions become germane:

WHAT EVENTS PRECIPITATED RAISING THE QUESTION OF THE PERSON'S POTENTIAL FOR VIOLENCE, AND IN WHAT CONTEXT DID THESE EVENTS TAKE PLACE?

It might be advantageous to be clear at the outset about precisely what the person did, or was alleged to have done, to have made someone (e.g., police officer, judge) concerned about his or her potential to be violent in the future, and the social context in which these events took place. A meticulous examination of the "precipitating incident" may yield much information of value to making a prediction. Knowing exactly who said or did what may provide clues to the situational contexts in which the individual reacts violently. Knowing, for example, that the assault of one person upon another took place in the context of a heated argument, but only after the victim had begun to cast aspersions upon the assailant's job performance, may raise the salience of job performance as an item worthy of further exploration. Thus, as Kozol (1975, p. 8) has written:

> Of paramount importance is a meticulous description of the actual assault. The potential for violent assaultiveness is the core of our diagnostic problem, and the description of the aggressor in action is often the most valuable single source of information. The patient's version is compared with the victim's version. In many cases we interview the victim ourselves. Our most serious errors in diagnosis have been made when we ignored the details in the description of the assault.

WHAT ARE THE PERSON'S RELEVANT DEMOGRAPHIC CHARACTERISTICS?

Among the first and easiest factors on which one can gather information are demographic ones. In which relevant groups associated in a positive or negative way with violent behavior does the individual hold membership? Earlier, evidence was reviewed on the relationship between several demographic variables and violent behavior: (a) *age* (violence peaking in the late teens and early 20s); (b) *sex* (males tending to be much more violent than females); (c) *race* (nonwhites, and particularly blacks, committing proportionately more "street" violence than whites); (d) *social class* (the lower the SES, the more likely the "street" violence); (e) *history of opiate or alcohol abuse* (violence being more likely if such a history is present); (f) *IQ* (the lower the estimated IQ, the more likely the violence; (g) *educational attainment* (the less the education, the more likely the violence); and (h) *residential and employment stability* (violence being more likely among those who move or change jobs frequently).

As noted previously, the inclusion of some predictive factors may make others worthless in the clinical context. Thus, among persons with an extensive history of past violence, the significance of race as a predictor is eliminated (see also the previous discussion of ethical issues).

WHAT IS THE PERSON'S HISTORY OF VIOLENT BEHAVIOR?

This is one of the most important questions one can ask in prediction, and obtaining a satisfactory answer may not be as easy as it seems. A very thorough probing of all forms of past violence should be conducted, paying particular attention to the *recency, severity,* and *frequency* of violent acts (Fisher, Brodsky, and Corse 1977). It should be noted whether the person's pattern of violent behavior appears to be escalating or declining. At least five indices of violence should be considered: (a) arrests and convictions for violent crimes; (b) juvenile court involvement for violent acts; (c) mental hospitalizations for "dangerous" behavior; (d) violence in the home, such as spouse and child abuse; and (e) other self-reported violent behavior such as bar fights, fights in school, arson, violent highway disputes, and perhaps violence toward animals. It should be noted in this regard that an *attempt* to kill often differs from an actual murder only by virtue of the former occurring in closer proximity to a hospital. Open-ended questions, such as "What is the most violent thing you have ever done?" and "What is the closest you have ever come to being violent?" may be helpful (American Psychiatric Association 1974).

WHAT IS THE BASE RATE OF VIOLENT BEHAVIOR AMONG INDIVIDUALS OF THIS PERSON'S BACKGROUND?

The importance of the base rate of violence as the most significant information one can obtain in making a prediction has been stressed several times. In some instances the base rate is published information (e.g., the Michigan study described in chapter 4 computed the base rate of violent crime among released prisoners to be 10.5 percent). In other cases, one can compute the base rate for oneself from available records (e.g., the base rate of violence on a mental hospital ward may be ascertained from a sample of hospital charts). In many circumstances, however, base rates are neither available nor readily obtainable. What is the base rate of violent behavior among persons referred by the police for civil commitment as "dangerous to others" on the basis of a recent overt act? Surely, it is not the same as the rate in the general population. Unless someone is willing to deny commitment to a portion of these persons to see how often, in fact, they are violent, their base rate will remain unknown.

What, then, is the clinician to do when confronted with the knowledge that the base rate is the most important single piece of information to have and yet he or she does not have it? One is left with Meehl's (1973) advice that, when actuarial data do not exist, we must use our heads. The clinician must estimate as reasonably, as judiciously, as wisely as possible what the approximate base rate would be. In so doing, one should always ask why the base rate of violence among persons similar to the person one is examining should be any higher than the general population rate. Having committed a recent overt act of violence, for example, may be one indicator that a higher-than-average base rate reasonably could be imputed to the individual.

WHAT ARE THE SOURCES OF STRESS IN THE PERSON'S CURRENT ENVIRONMENT?

WHAT COGNITIVE AND AFFECTIVE FACTORS INDICATE THAT THE PERSON MAY BE PREDISPOSED TO COPE WITH STRESS IN A VIOLENT MANNER?

WHAT COGNITIVE AND AFFECTIVE FACTORS INDICATE THAT THE PERSON MAY BE PREDISPOSED TO COPE WITH STRESS IN A NONVIOLENT MANNER?

One concept that may provide an organizing principle for many of the issues in violence prediction is that of stress. Stress can be understood as a state of imbalance between the demands of the social and physical environment and the capabilities of an individual to cope with these demands (McGrath 1970; Mechanic 1968). The higher the ratio of demands to resources, the more stress is experienced. Stress is thus to be thought of in terms of transactions between persons and their environments over time (Lazarus and Launier, in press). The voluminous literature on stress and its regulation has been masterfully systematized by Novaco (1979), to which the reader is referred for further information. Novaco presents a model of anger arousal as one form of reacting to stress, and his model, with some modification, may provide a vehicle for explicating many (but not all) of the factors to be assessed in violence prediction (cf. also Levinson and Ramsay 1979). It is presented in figure 2.

Stressful or aversive events such as frustrations, annoyances, insults, and assaults by another are seen in this model as filtered through certain cognitive processes in the individual who is the subject of assessment. Novaco conceptualizes these cognitive processes as being of two types: appraisals and expectations.

Appraisals refer to the manner in which an individual interprets an event as a provocation and therefore experiences it as aversive. Perceived intentionality is perhaps the clearest example of an antagonistic appraisal (e.g., "You didn't just bump into me, you *meant* to hit me."). How a person cognitively appraises an event may have a great influence on whether he or she ultimately responds to it in a violent manner. Some persons may be prone to interpret seemingly innocuous interactions as intentional slights. The chips on their shoulders may be precariously balanced.

Expectations are seen as cognitive processes that may influence the occurrence of violence in several ways. If one expects a desired outcome (e.g., a raise in pay, an expression of gratitude for a favor done) and it fails to occur, emotional arousal may

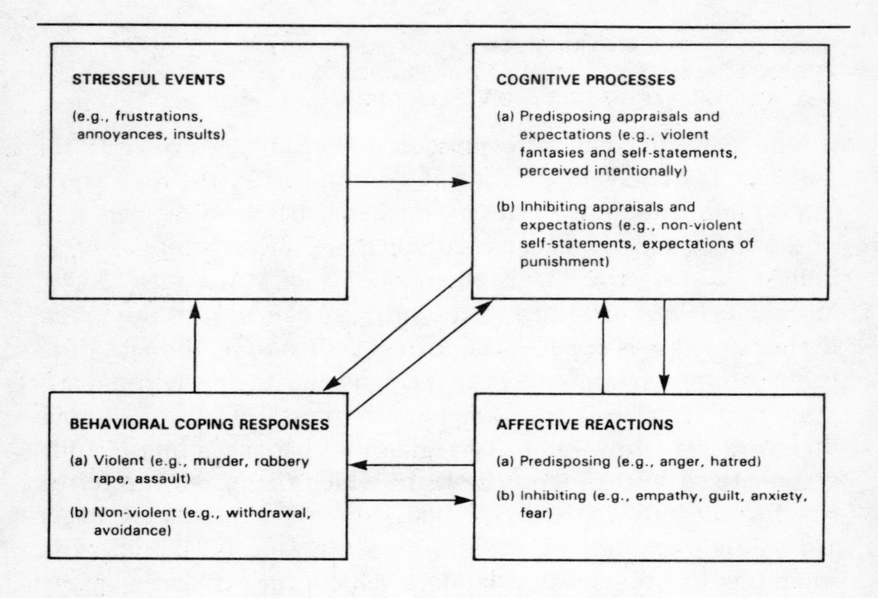

FIGURE 2: A Model of Some of the Factors To Be Assessed in the Prediction of Violent Behavior

ensue, and, depending upon the context, it may be perceived as anger. If one appraises an event as a provocation, the occurrence of violence may still depend upon whether one expects violence to be instrumental in righting the perceived wrong or whether one can expect violence to be met with a counterforce. One may, for example, regard having sand kicked in one's face as a deliberate affront and yet, upon learning that the agent of provocation is built like a football linebacker, have such low expectations for successful retaliation that violence is no longer under consideration. Alternatively, should the provocateur resemble Woody Allen, one's expectation that violence will prevail may rise accordingly.

Both expectations and appraisals may be reflected in the "private speech" or self-statements a person uses regarding violent behavior (e.g., "Anybody who insults my wife gets hit."). Violent delusions and fantasies may be thought of as extreme forms of such private conversations and statements of intention that are directly verbalized (i.e., threats of violence) may be particularly significant. For our purposes, appraisals and expectations may both be categorized as cognitive factors that "predispose" toward or "inhibit" violent behavior. These cognitive processes, in turn, may either give rise to certain affective or emotional reactions or may directly propel a behavioral response.

One need not be emotionally aroused to commit violent acts (e.g., the stereotypic "hitman" of *Godfather* fame). If, as is more typical, affective reactions are intervening, they may be viewed as either of a predisposing or an inhibiting type. Affective reactions predisposing a person toward violence would include the emotions of anger and hatred. While anger is not necessary for the occurrence of violent behavior, its arousal is a significant antecedent to aggression (Rule and Nesdale 1976). Fortunately, excellent work on the clinical assessment of anger is currently available (Novaco 1975, 1976, 1978, 1979). Affective reactions inhibiting violence (or, to put it more positively, predisposing toward peacefulness) include what have been called the "moral emotions" of empathy for the source of a frustration and guilt about injuring another, as well as anxiety reactions about engaging in violence or about the victim's possible retaliation. The lack of capacity for such affect has been viewed as the hallmark of the "sociopath" (Dinitz 1978).

In a state of alcohol or other drug-induced intoxication, many factors that ordinarily would serve to inhibit violence may be suppressed. The likelihood of such suppression should be estimated.

These affective reactions are then behaviorally expressed in terms of a coping response which, for our purposes, may be dichotomized as violent or nonviolent. The type of response chosen may go on to influence further stressful events, as would be the case when a divorce would eliminate interaction with a frustrating spouse or murder would precipitate the stresses of imprisonment. Whether or not a given coping response attenuates or exacerbates further life stresses would have relevance to whether a given level of violence potential could be expected to increase or decrease. As Toch (1969) emphasized, violence may be thought of as interactional in nature. If one person's coping response (e.g., insulting a person perceived as a threat) leads the other to escalate his or her provocations, violence may eventually ensue.

Several of the relationships expressed in figure 2 are *bidirectional* (as indicated by the arrows). This is meant to indicate that affective reactions can influence cognitive processes (e.g., "I feel so upset that I must be really angry") and that behavioral responses can affect both cognitions (e.g., "I hit him, therefore I must want to hurt him") and emotions (e.g., "I avoided her, therefore I must be angry at her").

The Novaco model of anger, as adapted here, is not exhaustive of the factors that influence violence. Demographic and historical factors, for example, are not addressed (hence, we inquire into them elsewhere in the assessment). But as a depiction of the cognitive and affective factors involved in violent behavior, the adapted Novaco model seems to capture well the essence of much of what must be assessed in violence prediction.

The kinds of stressors in which we are interested are those likely to be met with violent coping responses. While the kinds of stressors (e.g., frustrations, annoyances, insults, injuries) likely to result in violence are dependent upon the ways in which the individual cognitively and affectively processes them, and in fact may be thought of as fundamentally idiosyncratic in nature (see the next question), some general commonalities may exist among the kinds of situational demands likely to lead to violence. Based on the earlier analysis of the situational correlates of violent behavior (chapter 5), at least three broad areas of concern suggest themselves.

1. *Family stressors.* The frustrations and annoyances attendant to husband-wife and parent-child relationships, as many have noted, appear particularly susceptible to violent resolution. An assessment of the

individual's current living situation and the quality of social interactions involved would appear to be a priority endeavor.

2. *Peer group stressors.* Analogous to the family as a source of stress, the relationships of the individual to persons he or she considers, or until recently has considered, friends may be germane. In addition to disruption of friendship patterns being an instigator of stress, the role of peers as models for violent behavior (Bandura 1973, 1969) and as sources of social support for violent or nonviolent lifestyles (President's Commission on Mental Health 1978) suggests that peer relations be carefully investigated.
3. *Employment stressors.* While often overlooked, the stress associated with unemployment or with aversive employment situations may have a significant effect upon criminal behavior. These stressors may take the form of a recent firing, disputes with superiors or co-workers, or dissatisfaction with the nature of the work performed or the level of compensation paid for it.

HOW SIMILAR ARE THE CONTEXTS IN WHICH THE PERSON HAS USED VIOLENT COPING MECHANISMS IN THE PAST TO THE CONTEXTS IN WHICH THE PERSON LIKELY WILL FUNCTION IN THE FUTURE?

As described in chapter 5, the prediction model suggested by Bem and Funder (1978) would lead a clinician to assess two things: (a) the characteristics of the situations in which the person tends to react violently; and (b) the characteristics of the situations in which the person is likely to be functioning in the future. The third step (c) would then be to estimate the degree of similarity between these two kinds of situations. The more the similarity, the higher the probability of violent behavior occurring. It was noted that this approach is conducive to offering differential predictions, such as that the person has X probability of violence in situations typified by A, B, and C, and Y probability in situations typified by D, E, and F. Such predictions may prove useful in deciding among various forms of placement.

Another way of making the same point may be to reconstruct the pattern of violent behavior in the individual's past and to ascertain whether it is likely to repeat itself. Did the person become violent in the past when he or she was ending a relationship, or in a "manic" state, or unemployed for several months, or under the influence of alcohol or other drugs? Note that one is here individualizing the situational and personality bases for prediction. It is not that all people or even most people react violently in the given situations, but rather that this *particular* person, when confronted in the past with this *particular* constellation of events, has evidenced a pattern of violent behavior. Likewise for dispositional states: It is not that psychological disorder is associated with violence, but rather that this *particular* person, when experiencing this *particular* disorder, has tended to react violently in the past. While individualizing predictions in this manner may be a researcher's nightmare, it may also constitute an occasion in which the value of clinical judgment is maximized.

IN PARTICULAR, WHO ARE THE LIKELY VICTIMS OF THE PERSON'S VIOLENT BEHAVIOR, AND HOW AVAILABLE ARE THEY?

In line with the above, one may wish to single out for special attention the likely victims of a person's violent behavior. As an initial step, the demographic composition of the past-victim pool (e.g., women, the elderly) should be ascertained and, to the extent possible, an account constructed of the cognitive and affective factors motivating the individual to choose them rather than others as victims. For example, the past-victim pool may have been limited to males who cast aspersions upon the individual's sense of masculinity, to a particular person such as a spouse or child, or it may have been the indiscriminate choice of the next person encountered (Shah 1978*b*).

One would then wish to know how likely the environments in which the person will function in the future are to contain persons of similar characteristics. In situations in which a large class of persons forms the potential victim pool (e.g., women in the case of a rapist), there will surely be many persons at risk for potential victimization. But where only one or a small group of persons is the target of potential violence, the unavailability of those persons may preclude violent behavior. Thus, a father guilty of forced incest may desist from violence when his daughter is older. Removal of the potential victim (e.g., spouse or adolescent child) from the family through separating residences may decrease the frequency of interaction and, hence, the probability of violence.

In ascertaining the likely victims of an individual's violence, much attention should be given to those who are the expressed targets of fantasized, threatened, or planned violence, or who elicit strong negative emotions such as anger. In particular, it should be noted whether or not the potential victims are family members.

As Toch (1969) noted, the reaction of the potential victim of violence may distinguish a verbal altercation from a murder, and in certain circumstances this reaction may also be foreseeable (e.g., if the potential victim, as well as the potential offender, is likely to be armed).

WHAT MEANS DOES THE PERSON POSSESS TO COMMIT VIOLENCE?

As in the case of assessing suicide potential, the availability of lethal means of stress reduction may be noteworthy. Both the person's dispositional capability to do harm (e.g., physical strength, expertise in combat or the martial arts), and his or her proclivity to make use of access to external aids for harm infliction (e.g., guns, knives) should be inquired into. In particular, the recent acquisition of a weapon in furtherance of violent cognitions or in response to violent affect may be significant. The deluded person who has just bought a gun for protection against fantasized aggressors, or the easily enraged person who purchases a hunting knife to deter further annoyances, may require special attention.

SUMMARY

The 14 questions comprising a "reasonable guide to predicting violent behavior are presented in table 6.

After having considered these 14 questions, it would be appropriate for the clinician to review the answers obtained with four reliability questions:

Can I be sure that the information I have obtained is accurate?

TABLE 6 Question for the clinican in predicting violent behavior

1. Is it a prediction of violent behavior that is being requested?
2. Am I professionally competent to offer an estimate of the probability of future violence?
3. Are any issues of personal or professional ethics involved in this case?
4. Given my answers to the above questions, is this case an appropriate one in which to offer a prediction?
5. What events precipitated the question of the person's potential for violence being raised, and in what context did these events take place?
6. What are the person's relevent demographic characteristics?
7. What is the person's history of violent behavior?
8. What is the base rate of violent behavior among individuals of this person's background?
9. What are the sources of stress in the person's current environment?
10. What cognitive and affective factors indicate that the person may be predisposed to cope with stress in a nonviolent manner?
11. What cognitive and effective factors indicate that the person may be predisposed to cope with stress in a nonviolent manner?
12. How similar are the contexts in which the person has used violent coping mechanisms in the past to the contexts in which the person likely will function in the future?
13. In particular, who are the likely victims of the person's violent behavior, and how available are they?
14. What means does the person possess to commit violence?

It is advisable to corroborate as much of the information as possible. This can be done, within the limits of confidentiality and legality, by verifying the factors elicited in the clinical examination with other sources knowledgeable about particular facets of the case. The police may have the individual's arrest record, the hospital his or her commitment record, and a spouse or friend may confirm, refute, or add additional detail to what has been said by the individual being examined. Without such corroboration, the trustworthiness of the information upon which a decision is to be based may be questionable. "In this sense the telephone, the written request for past records, and the checking of information against other informants are the important diagnostic devices" (Scott 1977, p. 129).

While no formula can be offered as to how to score and combine what a person reveals on the various dimensions of the examination, the several admonitions given previously should be kept in mind during the process of arriving at a clinical estimate of violence potential. The following three questions may help in doing that.

Am I giving adequate attention to what I estimate the base rate of violent behavior to be among persons similarly situated to the person being examined?

What evidence do I have that the particular factors I have relied upon as predictors are in fact predictive of violent behavior? (e.g., are illusory correlations being avoided?)

Am I giving a balanced consideration to factors indicating the absence of violent behavior, as well as to factors indicating its occurrence?

In this last regard, particular attention should be paid to organizational contingencies and their associated demand characteristics which may bias clinical assessments in a conservative "better safe than sorry" direction.

Finally, while professional peer review is becoming accepted practice for psychiatric or psychological treatment, there appears to be less emphasis on the peer review of clinical assessments. The development of some formal means for obtaining the opinion of colleagues in difficult cases of violence prediction appears a highly worthwhile endeavor. How do others rate the sources of stress in the person's environment? What is their best estimate of the relevant base rates? Consultation with colleagues on such issues may do much to improve the reliability of clinical predictions of violent behavior and may be a source of mutual professional education.

A CASE STUDY

To illustrate how the questions presented above might be used to facilitate the clinical examination of a given case, a case will be described, the questions answered, and a report presented. The case is hypothetical. It should be noted that the examination and report are for the purpose of predicting violent behavior *only.* Additional issues that are often addressed by a mental health professional, such as the presence of psychological disorder or recommendations concerning treatment, are not considered (See Roth 1978). The examination and report should be modified to consider such questions when they are of concern.

The case is that of Mr. Smith, a person who was civilly committed as "dangerous to others" under an emergency commitment statute, and who, several days later, desires his release on the grounds that he is not, in fact, "dangerous." The hospital staff, believing otherwise, wishes to have him remain in the hospital for an additional period of treatment. A judge requests a mental health professional not on the hospital staff to assess the individual's potential for violent behavior and to submit a report of the findings. The specific facts of the case are as follows.

Mr. Smith is a 20-year-old male who has never married and who dropped out of school in the ninth grade. His IQ is estimated to be in the dull-normal range. He has been residentially unstable, living at six different addresses since being discharged from the Marines 2 years ago.

The police report accompanying the commitment form states that they received a call from an employee of the NT company saying that Mr. Smith had gone "berserk" and was threatening his supervisor. When the police arrived they found Mr. Smith with a crowbar in his hand threatening to kill Mr. Brown, his supervisor. Mr. Smith appeared to be either drunk or otherwise "high" and was described as "incoherent and bizarre." When Mr. Smith broke the window of the office into which Mr. Brown had fled, the police forcibly subdued him.

During the evaluation interview, Mr. Smith stated that Mr. Brown had told him when he was hired, he could progress rapidly through the ranks of the company. At the time of the incident, 1 month after being hired, Mr. Smith was still on the assembly line and felt that he had been deceived. When Mr. Brown criticized Mr. Smith for arriving at work several hours late and being in a state of intoxication, Mr. Smith became enraged. Thereupon, Mr. Brown fired him, and Mr. Smith picked up the crowbar.

Mr. Smith appeared very frustrated that he has not achieved a higher level of responsibility at his job. He wanted both the prestige and money that would go with advancement and felt cheated that he has not received them.

During the interview, Mr. Smith stated that he would like to get even with Mr. Brown, and that he would love to get him alone for just 5 minutes. He stated that he had thought about nothing else while in the hospital and that he did not know how he could give Mr. Brown "what he has coming to him" other than by physically assaulting him.

Mr. Smith appeared very agitated at the mention of Mr. Brown's name and readily volunteered that he was still enraged at how Mr. Brown had treated him.

Mr. Smith stated that he did not want to go to jail or return to the hospital for injuring Mr. Brown. He also stated that he realized Mr. Brown "had a job to get done" at the plant but that he did not think his arriving late for work on occasion should bother Mr. Brown as much as it did. He stated that he felt sorry that he had threatened some of his co-workers in his attempt to reach Mr. Brown.

His police record revealed that Mr. Smith had been arrested three times during the past 4 years, once for aggravated assault, once for simple assault, and once for public intoxication. He received a suspended sentence for the first incident, charges were modified to "disturbing the peace" in the second incident, and he served a few days in the county jail on the final charge. When asked to describe the previous assaults, he stated someone tried to "push me around and put me down in front of my friends." He admitted that he had been drinking heavily prior to both assaults.

Now let us apply the questions to the clinician in this case.

Is it a prediction of violent behavior that is being requested?

I am clearly being requested to offer an assessment of the likelihood of violent behavior to others and not, for example, of competence to stand trial or criminal responsibility.

Am I professionally competent to offer an estimate of the probability of future violence?

In addition to being knowledgeable about the general topic of the clinical prediction of violent behavior (e.g., I have read the American Psychiatric Association (1974) report, Kozol et al. 1972; Cohen et al. 1978), I have just read Monahan's monograph on the prediction of violent behavior and several current articles on the topic in professional journals. I recently attended a continuing education seminar on civil commitment procedures in my State and believe I understand them. I am unaware of personal biases that would compromise my abilities to evaluate this case. In all, I believe that offering a prediction in a case like this is within the realm of mental health expertise and that I am professionally competent to do so.

Are there any issues of personal or professional ethics involved in this case?

To participate in a short-term civil commitment decision does not threaten to compromise my ethical integrity, nor are the factors I will clinically rely upon to predict violent behavior in this case morally problematic.

I *am* bothered by the fact that neither statutory nor case law provides me with a definition of violent behavior, a statement of the time frame of concern, or a threshold probability of violence necessary to invoke civil commitment. Therefore, I will specify that what I am predicting is "serious, unjustified bodily harm" within the next 2 weeks, and I will simply state the probability figure I arrive at. It will then be up to the judge to do with this information what he or she will.

Given my answers to the above questions, is this case an appropriate one in which to offer a prediction?

Offering a prediction in this case does indeed appear to be appropriate.

What events precipitated the question of the person's potential for violence being raised, and in what context did these events take place?

He was picked up by the police for threatening his supervisor. This took place while the examinee was intoxicated and after he had been reprimanded for poor work performance.

What are the person's relevant demographic characteristics?

He is a 20-year-old, never-married male high school dropout. His IQ is dull-normal. He has a history of alcohol problems but no involvement with other drugs. His residential and employment history have been unstable.

What is the person's history of violent behavior?

His history, with two arrests for violent acts in addition to the current incident, is fairly extensive.

What is the base rate of violent behavior among individual's of this person's background?

To my knowledge (and I have sought such information), no base rates of violent behavior among persons with whom I would group Mr. Smith are available. Extrapolating from the most relevant pieces of research and based on my own clinical experience, my best estimate of the base rate of violent behavior among persons such as Mr. Smith is in the range of 30 percent.

What are the sources of stress in the person's current environment?

He is frustrated at not being able to achieve unrealistically high job advancement with little effort on his part. He feels bitter and cheated by his lack of advancement and attributes responsibility for this to Mr. Brown.

What cognitive and affective factors indicate that the person may be predisposed to cope with stress in a violent manner?

He is in an acute state of emotional arousal which he labels as anger. He readily expresses violent fantasies toward Mr. Brown.

What cognitive and affective factors indicate that the person may be predisposed to cope with stress in a nonviolent manner?

He expresses fear of being institutionalized if he assaults Mr. Brown and some empathy for his co-workers who were threatened during the precipitating incident.

How similar are the contexts in which the person has used violent coping mechanisms in the past to the contexts in which the person likely will function in the future?

Mr. Smith's past assaultive behavior occurred in contexts that could be characterized as including the presence of an authority figure, a reprimand or humiliation in the presence of peers, and a state of intoxication on the part of Mr. Smith. These factors are likely to be present in the immediate future, since Mr. Smith is intent on returning to his former place of employment to confront Mr. Brown as soon as he is released.

In particular, who are the likely victims of the person's violent behavior, and how available are they?

Plainly, Mr. Brown is the likely victim, and both his place of work and home address are known to Mr. Smith.

What means does the person possess to commit violence?

Mr. Smith, as an ex-Marine, is trained in methods of assault.

A CLINICAL REPORT

The following is the form a report might take based upon the above examination:

Judge Jane Doe
County Court House

Dear Judge Doe:

This letter reports my evaluation of the likelihood that Mr. J. Smith (Case No. 1234) will inflict serious bodily harm upon another person during the next 2-week period. This evaluation was done in response to the Court's request for information relevant to the issue of whether Mr. Smith's petition for release from the County Medical Center Psychiatric Unit should be granted. Mr. Smith has been involuntarily committed for a 72-hour observation period under Section 5150, and the hospital wishes to continue his commitment for an additional 14 days of intensive treatment. Mr. Smith, through his attorney, contests the allegation that he constitutes a continuing "danger to others."

I interviewed Mr. Smith at the Medical Center for approximately 2 hours on Monday, August 14. I informed him of the purpose of the examination before it began. I also read Mr. Smith's hospital records and the written police report on him. I discussed Mr. Smith's case with the ward staff.

Mr. Smith is a 20-year-old, never-married, male who appears to be of dull-normal intelligence. He has been intermittently employed as a factory worker since dropping out of high school in the ninth grade several years ago. At the time of his commitment, he had been working on the assembly line at the N T company for a period of 1 month.

His police record reveals that he has been arrested three times during the past 4 years–once for aggravated assault, once for simple assault, and once for public intoxication. He received a suspended sentence for the first incident, charges were modified to disturbing the peace in the second incident, and he served several days in the County Jail on the final charge. His hospital record reveals no prior hospitalization. He admits to several school suspensions for fighting and several barroom altercations that did not result in an arrest.

The police report filed for the incident precipitating his commitment states that the police responded to a call from a supervisor at the N T company on Friday, August 11. When they arrived they found Mr. Smith with a crowbar in his hand threatening to kill a Mr. Brown, his foreman. Mr. Brown had barricaded himself into an office. Mr. Smith appeared to the officers to be intoxicated from alcohol or some other substance and his screaming at Mr. Brown was described as "incoherent" and "bizarre." The officers failed to talk him into putting down the metal bar, and, when he broke the window on the door of the office into which Mr. Brown had fled, the police forcibly subdued him and brought him to the Medical Center.

During the interview, Mr. Smith was clearly upset at the incident. He raised his voice frequently and began to pace the room. He stated that Mr. Brown had told him when he was hired that he could progress through the ranks of the company "all the way to the top," if he had the ability and the energy. Now, 1 month later, he was still on the assembly line "going nowhere." He blamed Mr. Brown for his predicament and said that Mr. Brown was deliberately "holding me down" so that his superior talents would go unnoticed and not become a source of competition to Mr. Brown himself. When Mr. Brown criticized Mr. Smith for arriving at work several hours late and appearing in a state of intoxication, Mr. Smith states that he "just saw red" and told the foreman that he could do a better job drunk and in half the time than the foreman could ever do. Mr. Brown thereupon fired Mr. Smith and ordered him out of the plant. At that point, Mr. Smith said that he 'went wild" and began chasing Mr. Brown with the iron bar.

During the interview, Mr. Smith repeatedly and with much anger referred to his former foreman as "that son of a bitch." He states that Mr. Brown "has not heard the end of this–not by a long shot" and that "nobody makes a fool of me and gets away with it." When asked directly whether he intended to harm Mr. Brown, Mr. Smith was evasive and would only reply "we'll see, we'll see." He intends to confront Mr.

Brown at his first opportunity. He denied owning a gun but stated that he had easy access to the gun of a friend. The ward staff confirmed his state of acute agitation.

Based upon the above data, in particular upon his demographic profile, his history of violent behavior including a recent overt act of violence, his currently stressful employment situation, his alcohol-suppressed inhibitions, and his acute and clearly unresolved hostility toward Mr. Brown, it is my professional opinion that Mr. Smith is more likely than not to inflict serious bodily harm upon another person within the next 2-week period. That other person is likely to be Mr. Brown.

CONCLUSION

A study recently published in the *Stanford Law Review* (Wise 1978) surveyed over 1,200 psychologists and psychiatrists in California concerning the issue of "dangerous behavior." Eighty percent of the responding mental health professionals saw at least one patient per year whom they considered to be "potentially dangerous." The mean number of "potentially dangerous" patients seen per year was 14. Despite the prevalence of violence prediction as an issue of clinical concern—arising an average of more than once per month for psychiatrists and psychologists throughout the State—the clinicians "found it difficult to articulate their standards. Typically, they said that they based their decisions on 'clinical judgment that the threat was serious' or that they 'believed' the patient was 'clearly dangerous' and likely to 'act on the threat' (78.2% of those stating their criteria)" (p. 181).

It was to assist in articulating standards that this monograph was written. Yet, even those most adept at prediction will be hard pressed not to let themselves be influenced by the contingencies operating in the clinical situation. The Stanford survey tried to assess the effects of the *Tarasoff* decision—that psychiatrists and psychologists may be liable for the violent acts of patients they predict, or *should* predict, to be violent—on the clinical practice of the 1,200 therapists who responded to their survey.

One-quarter of the therapists who responded to the survey said that they were now giving more attention in their therapy sessions to the possibility of their patients' violent behavior. Almost as many said that the ruling led them to focus more frequently on less serious threats made by their patients. One-third of the psychiatrists and psychologists surveyed increased the frequency with which they consulted with colleagues concerning cases in which violence was an issue, and over half reported an increase in their own anxiety concerning the entire topic of "dangerousness" as a result of the *Tarasoff* decision. Unfortunately, the survey also revealed that as a result of *Tarasoff* almost one-fifth of the respondents had decided to *avoid* asking questions that could yield information bearing on the likelihood of violent behavior by their patients. Even more reported that they had changed their recordkeeping procedures in an effort to avoid legal liability they might otherwise incur as a result of *Tarasoff.* "Some therapists ceased keeping detailed records; others began keeping *more* detailed records, including information that might justify any decisions they made and thereby trying to create a favorable evidentiary record for future litigation" (Wise, 1978, p. 182).

The prediction of violent behavior is difficult under the best of circumstances. It becomes more so when powerful social contingencies pull and push the clinician now in one direction, then in another. But such is likely to be the case for the foreseeable future, until the patient's right not to be a false positive and the victim's right not to be set upon by a false negative are balanced in the courts and legislatures of the land.

REFERENCES

Ajzen, I. Intuitive theories of events and the effects of base-rate information on prediction. *Journal of Personality and Social Psychology,* 1977, *35,* 303-314.

American Psychiatric Association. *Clinical aspects of the violent individual.* Washington, D.C.: American Psychiatric Association, 1974.

American Psychological Association. Report of the Task Force on the Role of Psychology in the Criminal Justice System. *American Psychologist,* 1978, *33,* 1099-1113.

Arthur, R. Success is predictable. *Military Medicine,* 1971, *136,* 539-545.

Ashley, M. Outcome of 1,000 cases paroled from the Middletown State Homeopathic Hospital. *State Hospital Quarterly,* 1922, *8,* 64-70.

Bandura, A. *Principles of Behavior Modification.* New York: Holt, Rinehart & Winston, 1969.

Bandura, A. *Aggression: A Social Learning Analysis.* Englewood Cliffs, N.J.: Prentice-Hall, 1973.

Bard, M. Family intervention police teams as a community mental health resource. *Journal of Criminal Law, Criminology and Police Science,* 1969, *60,* 247-250.

Barker, R. *Ecological Psychology: Concepts and Methods for Studying the Environment of Human Behavior.* Palo Alto: Stanford University Press, 1968.

Bartlett, C., and Green, L. Clinical prediction: Does one sometimes know too much? *Journal of Counseling Psychology,* 1966, *13,* 267-270.

Baxstrom v. *Herold.* 383 U.S. 107, 1966.

Beck, A., Resnick, H., and Lettieri, D. *The Prediction of Suicide.* Bowie, Md.: Charles, 1974.

Bem, D., and Allen, A. On predicting some of the people some of the time: The search for cross-situational consistencies in behavior. *Psychological Review,* 1974, *81,* 506-520.

Bem, D., and Funder, D. Predicting more of the people more of the time: Assessing the personality of situations. *Psychological Review,* 1978, *85,* 485-501.

Berkowitz, L., and LePage, A. Weapons as aggression-eliciting stimuli. *Journal of Personality and Social Psychology,* 1967, 202-207.

Block, J. *The Q-Sort Method in Personality Assessment and Psychiatric Research.* Springfield, Ill.: Thomas, 1961.

Boland, P., and Wilson, J. Age, crime and punishment. *The Public Interest,* 1978, *51,* 22-34.

Bolton, A. "A Study of the Need for and Availability of Mental Health Services for Mentally Disordered Jail Inmates and Juveniles in Detention Facilities." Unpublished report, Arthur Bolton Associates, Boston, Mass., 1976.

Brenner, M. Does employment cause crime? *Criminal Justice Newsletter,* Oct. 24, 1977, p. 5.

Brill, H., and Malzberg, B. "Statistical Report on the Arrest Record of Male Ex-Patients, Age 16 and Over, Released From New York State Mental Hospitals During the Period 1946-48. Unpublished manuscript, New York State Department of Mental Hygiene, 1954.

Brodsky, S. *Psychologists in the Criminal Justice System.* Urbana, Ill.: University of Illinois Press, 1973.

Buss, A. *Psychology of Aggression.* New York: Wiley, 1961.

Campbell, D., and Stanley, J. *Experimental and Quasi-Experimental Design for Research.* Chicago: Rand McNalley, 1966.

Carroll, J. Judgements of recidivism risk: The use of base-rate information in parole decisions. In: Lipsitt, P., and Sales, B., eds. *New Directions in Psycholegal Research.* New York: Van Nostrand, 1980.

Chapman, L., and Chapman, J. Illusory correlations as an obstacle to the use of valid psychodiagnostic signs. *Journal of Abnormal Psychology,* 1969, *74,* 271-280.

Cocozza, J.; Melick, M.; and Steadman, H. Trends in violent crime among ex-mental patients. *Criminology,* 1978, *16,* 317-334.

Cocozza, J.; and Steadman, H. Some refinements in the measurement and prediction of dangerous behavior. *American Journal of Psychiatry,* 1974, 1012-1020.

Cocozza, J., and Steadman, H. The failure of psychiatric predictions of dangerousness: Clear and convincing evidence. *Rutgers Law Review,* 1976, *29,* 1084-1101.

Cocozza, J., and Steadman, H. Prediction in psychiatry: An example of misplaced confidence in experts. *Social Problems,* 1978, *25,* 265-276.

Cohen, L., and Freeman, H. How dangerous to the community are state hospital patients? *Connecticut State Medical Journal,* 1945, *9,* 697-700.

Cohen, M.; Groth, A.; and Siegel, R. The clinical prediction of dangerousness. *Crime and Delinquency,* Jan. 1978, 28-39.

Cook, P. The correctional carrot: Better jobs for parolees. *Policy Analysis,* 1975, *1,* 11-54.

Cross v. *Harris,* 418 F.2d. 1095, 1969.

Department of Justice. *Criminal Victimization in the United States.* Washington, D.C.: Supt. of Docs., U.S. Print. Off., 1978.

Dershowitz, A. Psychiatrists' power in civil commitment. *Psychology Today,* 1969, *2,* 43-47.

Dershowitz, A. Preventive confinement: A suggested framework for constitutional analysis. *Texas Law Review,* 1973, *51,* 1277-1324.

Dershowitz, A. The origins of preventive confinement in Anglo-American law. Part I: The English experience. *University of Cincinnati Law Review,* 1974, *43,* 1-60.

Diamond, B. The psychiatric prediction of dangerousness. *University of Pennsylvania Law Review,* 1974, *123,* 439-452.

Dinitz, S. Chronically antisocial offenders. In: Conrad, J., Dinitz, S. *In Fear of Each Other: Studies of Dangerousness in America.* Lexington, Mass: Lexington Books, 1978, pp. 21-42.

Dix, G. Determining the continued dangerousness of psychologically abnormal sex offenders. *Journal of Psychiatry and the Law,* 1975, *3,* 327-344.

Dix, G. "Civil" commitment of the mentally ill and the need for data on the prediction of dangerousness. *American Behavioral Scientists,* 1976, *19,* 318-334.

Dix, G. Administration of the Texas death penalty statutes: Constitutional infirmities related to the prediction of dangerousness. *Texas Law Review,* 1977*a, 55,* 1343-1414.

Dix, G. The death penalty, "dangerousness," psychiatric testimony, and professional ethics. *American Journal of Criminal Law,* 1977*b, 5,* 151-204.

Dixon v. *Attorney General of the Commonwealth of Pennsylvania,* 325 F. Supp. 966, 1971.

Driscoll, J.; Meyer, R.; and Schanie, C. Training police in family crisis intervention, *Journal of Applied Behavioral Science,* 1973, *9,* 62-82.

Durbin, J.; Pasewark, R.; and Albers, D. Criminality and mental illness. A study of arrest rates in a rural state. *American Journal of Psychiatry,* 1977, *134,* 80-83.

Elstein, A. Clinical judgment: Psychological research and medical practice. *Science,* 1976, *194,* 696-700.

Endler, N., and Magnusson, D. Toward an interactional psychology of personality. *Psychological Bulletin,* 1976, *83,* 956-974.

Ennis, B., and Emery, R. *The Rights of Mental Patients–An American Civil Liberties Union Handbook.* New York: Avon, 1978.

Ervin, F., and Lion, J. Clinical evaluation of the violent patient. In: Mulvihill, D., and Tumin, M., eds. *Crimes of Violence: Staff Report Submitted to the National Commission on the Causes and Prevention of Violence.* Vol. 13. Washington, D.C.: Supt. of Docs., U.S. Print. Off., 1969.

Fairweather, G.; Sanders, D.; and Tornatzky, L. *Creating Change in Mental Health Organizations.* New York: Pergamon Press, 1974.

Farmer, L. "Observation and Study: Critique and Recommendations on Federal Procedures." Unpublished report, Federal Judicial Center, Washington, D.C., 1977.

Federal Aviation Agency. *Aviation Weather for Pilots and Flight Operations Personnel.* Washington, D.C.: Supt. of Docs., U.S. Print. Off., 1965.

Fisher, B.; Brodsky, S.; and Corse, S. "Monitoring and Classification Guidelines and Procedures." Unpublished manuscript. Center for Correctional Psychology, Department of Psychology, University of Alabama, 1977.

Fisher, R. "Factors Influencing the Prediction of Dangerousness: Authoritarianism, Dogmatism, and Data Quantity." Unpublished doctoral dissertation, Department of Psychology, University of Alabama, 1976.

Forst, M. The psychiatric evaluation of dangerousness in two trial court jurisdictions. *The Bulletin of the American Academy of Psychiatry and the Law,* 1977, *9,* 98-110.

Frodi, A.; Macauley, J.; and Thorne, P. Are women always less agressive than men? A review of the experimental literature. *Psychological Bulletin,* 1977, *84,* 634-660.

Geis, G., and Meier, R. Looking backward and forward: Criminologists on criminology and a career. *Criminology,* 1978, *16,* 273-288.

Geis, G., and Monahan, J. The social ecology of violence. In: Lickona, T., ed. *Moral Development and Behavior: Theory, Research, and Social Issues.* New York: Holt, Rinehart & Winston, 1976, pp. 342-356.

Geller, J., and Lister, E. The process of criminal commitment for pretrial psychiatric examination: An evaluation. *American Journal of Psychiatry*, 1978, *135*, 53-60.

Giovannoni, J., and Gurel, L. Socially disruptive behavior of ex-mental patients. *Archives of General Psychiatry*, 1967, *17*, 146-153.

Glaser, D. *The Effectiveness of a Prison and Parole System.* Indianapolis: Bobbs-Merrill, 1964.

Glueck, S., and Glueck, E. *Unraveling Juvenile Delinquency.* New York: The Commonwealth Fund, 1950.

Goldstein, R. Brain research and violent behavior. *Archives of Neurology*, 1974, *30*, 1-18.

Gordon, R. A critique of the evaluation of Patuxent Institution, with particular attention to the issues of dangerousness and recidivism. *Bulletin of the American Academy of Psychiatry and the Law*, 1977, *5*, 210-255.

Gottfredson, D.; Wilkins, L.; and Hoffman, P. *Guidelines for Parole and Sentencing.* Lexington, Mass: Lexington Books, 1978.

Greenland, C. "The Prediction and Management of Dangerous Behavior: Social Policy Issues." Law and Psychiatry Symposium, Clarke University, 1978.

Guttmacher, M. In: Rappaport, J., ed. *The Clinical Evaluation of the Dangerousness of the Mentally Ill.* Springfield, Ill.: Charles C Thomas, 1967.

Guze, S. *Criminality and Psychiatric Disorders.* New York: Oxford University Press, 1976.

Halatyn, T. "Violence Prediction Using Actuarial Methods: A Review and Prospectus." Unpublished manuscript, National Council on Crime and Delinquency, Davis, Calif., 1975.

Halleck, S. *Psychiatry and the Dilemmas of Crime.* New York: Harper & Row, 1967.

Hamparian, D., Schuster, R., Dinitz, S., and Conrad, J. *The Violent Few: A Study of Dangerous Juvenile Offenders.* Lexington, Mass: Lexington Books, 1978.

Hanley, C. Problems in the estimation of delinquency potential. In Toch, H., ed. *The Psychology of Crime and Criminal Justice.* New York: Holt, Rinehart & Winston, 1979.

Hartogs, R. Who will act violently: The predictive criteria. In: Hartogs, R., and Artzt, E., eds. *Violence: The Causes and Solution.* New York: Dell, 1970.

Hartshorne, H., and May, M. *Studies in the Nature of Character.* New York: Macmillan, 1928.

Heller, K., and Monahan, J. *Psychology and Community Change.* Homewood, Ill.: Dorsey Press, 1977.

Hellman, D., and Blackman, N. Enuresis, firesetting, and cruelty to animals: A triad predictive of adult crime. *American Journal of Psychiatry*, 1966, *122*, 1431-1435.

Heumann, M. *Plea Bargaining: The Experience of Prosecutors, Judges, and Defense Attorneys.* Chicago: University of Chicago Press, 1978.

Hindelang, M. *Criminal Victimization in Eight American Cities.* Cambridge, Mass: Ballinger, 1976.

Hindelang, M. Race and involvement in crimes. *American Sociological Review*, 1978, *43*, 93-109.

Hirschi, T., and Hindelang, M. Intelligence and delinquency: A revisionist review. *American Sociological Review*, 1977, *42*, 571-587.

Hoffman, P., Gottfredson, D., Wilkins, L., and Pasela, G. The operational use of an experience table. *Criminology*, 1974, *12*, 214-228.

Holt, R. *Methods in Clinical Psychology. Volume 2: Prediction and Research.* New York: Plenum, 1978.

Jurek v. *Texas,* 96 S.Ct. 2950, 1976.

Justice, B., Justice, R., and Kraft, J. Early warning signs of violence: Is a triad enough? *American Journal of Psychiatry,* 1974, *131,* 457-459.

Kahle, L., and Sales, B. Due process of law and the attitudes of professionals toward involuntary civil commitment. In: Lipsitt, P., and Sales, B., ed. *New Directions in Psycholegal Research.* New York: Van Nostrand Reinhold, 1980.

Kahneman, D., and Tversky, D. On the psychology of prediction. *Psychological Review,* 1973, *81,* 237-251.

Kastermeier, R., and Eglit, H. Parole release decision-making: Rehabilitation, expertise, and the demise of mythology. *American University Law Review,* 1973, *22,* 477-1137.

Kelley, C. *Uniform Crime Reports–1977.* F.B.I. Washington, D.C.: Supt. of Docs., U.S. Print. Off., 1977.

Kelly, J. Ecological constraints on mental health services. *American Psychologist,* 1966, *21,* 535-539.

Konečni, V., Mulcahy, E., and Ebbesen, E. Prison or mental hospital: Factors affecting the processing of persons suspected of being "mentally disordered sex offenders." In: Lipsitt, P., and Sales, B., eds. *New Directions in Psycholegal Research.* New York: Van Nostrand Reinhold, 1980.

Kozol, H. The diagnosis of dangerousness. In: Pasternack, S., ed. *Violence and Victims.* New York: Spectrum, 1975, pp. 3-13.

Kozol, H., Boucher, R., and Garofalo, R. The diagnosis and treatment of dangerousness. *Crime and Delinquency,* 1972, *18,* 371-392.

Kozol, H., Boucher, R., and Garofalo, R. Dangerousness: A reply to Monahan. *Crime and Delinquency,* 1973, *19,* 554-555.

Kuhn, T. *The Structure of Scientific Revolutions.* Chicago: University of Chicago Press, 1962.

Lagos, J., Perlmutter, K., and Saexinger, H. Fear of the mentally ill: Empirical support for the common man's response. *American Journal of Psychiatry,* 1977, *134,* 1134-1137.

Lazarus, R., and Launier, R. Stress-related transactions between persons and environment. In: Pervin, L., and Lewis, M., eds. *Internal and External Determinants of Behavior.* New York: Plenum, in press.

Levine, D. The concept of dangerousness: Criticism and Compromise. In: Sales, B., ed. *Psychology in the Legal Process.* New York: Spectrum, 1977, pp. 147-162.

Levine, J. The potential for crime overreporting in criminal victimization surveys. *Criminology,* 1976, *14,* 307-330.

Levinson, R., and Ramsay, G. Dangerousness, stress, and mental health evaluations. *Journal of Health and Social Behavior, 20,* 1979, 178-187.

Lewin, K., Lippett, R., and White, R. Patterns of aggressive behavior in experimentally created "social climates." *Journal of Social Psychology,* 1939, *10,* 271-299.

Lefkowitz, M., Eron, L., Walder, L., and Heusmann, L. *Growing Up To Be Violent.* New York: Pergamon, 1977.

Livermore, J., Malmquist, C., and Meehl, P. On the justifications for civil commitment. *University of Pennsylvania Law Review,* 1968, *117,* 75-96.

Loftus, E., and Monahan, J. Trial by data: Psychological research as legal evidence. *American Psychologist,* 1980, *35,* 270-283.

Maccoby, E., and Jacklin, C. *The Psychology of Sex Differences.* Stanford: Stanford University Press, 1974.

MacDonald, J. Homicidal threats. *American Journal of Psychiatry,* 1967, *124,* 475.

McCord, J. Some child rearing antecedents to criminal behavior in adult men. *Journal of Personality and Social Psychology,* 1979, *37,* 1477-1486.

McGrath, J. *Social and Psychological Factors in Stress.* New York: Holt, Rinehart & Winston, 1970.

McGuire, J. "Prediction of Dangerous Behavior in a Federal Correctional Institution." Unpublished dissertation. Department of Psychology. Florida State University, 1976.

Mechanic, D. *Medical Sociology: A Selective View.* New York: Free Press, 1968.

Meehl, P. *Clinical Versus Statistical Prediction: A Theoretical Analysis and a Review of the Evidence.* Minneapolis, University of Minnesota Press, 1954.

Meehl, P. *Psychodiagnosis: Selected papers.* Minneapolis, University of Minnesota Press, 1973.

Meehl, P., and Rosen, A. Antecedent probability and the efficacy of psychometric signs, patterns, or cutting scores. *Psychological Bulletin,* 1955, *52,* 194-216.

Megargee, E. The psychology of violence. In: Mulvihill, D., and Tumin, M., eds. *Crimes of Violence: A Staff Report Submitted to the National Commission on the Causes and Prevention of Violence.* Washington, D.C.: Supt. of Docs., U.S. Gov. Print. Off., 1969, *13,* 1037-1016.

Megargee, E. The prediction of violence with psychological tests. In: Spielberger, C., ed. *Current Topics in Clinical and Community Psychology.* New York: Academic Press, 1970.

Megargee, E. Recent research on overcontrolled and undercontrolled personality patterns among violent offenders. *Sociological Symposium,* 1973, *9,* 37-50.

Megargee, E. The prediction of dangerous behavior. *Criminal Justice and Behavior,* 1976, *3,* 3-21.

Mental Health Law Project. Suggested statute on civil commitment. *Mental Disability Law Reporter,* 1977, *2,* 127-159.

Millard v. *Harris,* 406 F.2d 964, 1968.

Mischel, W. *Personality and Assessment.* New York: Wiley, 1968.

Mischel, W. Toward a cognitive social learning reconceptualization of personality. *Psychological Review,* 1973, *80,* 252-283.

Monahan, J. Dangerous offenders: A critique of Kozol, et al. *Crime and Delinquency,* 1973, *19,* 418-420.

Monahan, J. The prevention of violence. In: Monahan, J., ed. *Community Mental Health and the Criminal Justice System.* New York: Pergamon Press, 1976, 13-34.

Monahan, J. Empirical analyses of civil commitment: Critique and context. *Law and Society Review,* 1977*b,* *11,* 619-628.

Monahan, J. Strategies for an empirical analysis of the prediction of violence in civil commitment. *Law and Human Behavior,* 1977*a,* *1,* 363-371.

Monahan, J. Prediction research and the emergency commitment of dangerous mentally ill persons: A reconsideration. *American Journal of Psychiatry,* 1978*b,* *135,* 198-201.

Monahan, J. The prediction of violent criminal behavior: A methodological critique and prospectus. In: Blumstein, A., Cohen, J.; and Nagin, D., eds. *Deterrence and Incapacitation: Estimating the Effects of Criminal Sanctions on Crime Rates.* Washington, D.C.: National Academy of Sciences, 1978*a*, 244-269.

Monahan, J., ed. *Who Is the Client? The Ethics of Psychological Intervention in the Criminal Justice System.* Washington, D.C.: American Psychological Association, 1980.

Monahan, J., and Catalano, R. Toward the safe society: Police agencies and environmental planning. *Journal of Criminal Justice,* 1976, *4,* 1-7.

Monahan, J., Caldeira, C., and Friedlander, H. The police and the mentally ill. A comparison of arrested and committed persons. *International Journal of Law and Psychiatry,* 1979, *2,* 509-518.

Monahan, J., and Cummings, L. The prediction of dangerousness as a function of its perceived consequences. *Journal of Criminal Justice,* 1975, *2,* 239-242.

Monahan, J., and Geis, G. Controlling "dangerous" people, *Annals of the American Academy of Political and Social Science,* 1976, *423,* 142-151.

Monahan, J., and Hood, G. Ascriptions of dangerousness; The eye (and age, sex, education, location, and politics) of the beholder. In: Simon, R., ed. *Research in Law and Sociology.* Greenwich, Conn.: Johnson, 1978, 143-151.

Monahan, J., and Monahan, L. Prediction research and the role of psychologists in correctional institutions. *San Diego Law Review,* 1977, *14,* 1028-1038.

Monahan, J., and Novaco, R. Corporate violence: A psychological analysis. In: Lipsitt, P., and Sales, B., ed. *New Directions in Psycholegal Research.* New York: Van Nostrand, 1980.

Monahan, J., Novaco, R., and Geis, G. Corporate violence: Research strategies for community psychology. In: Sarbin, T., ed. *Challenges to the Criminal Justice System.* New York: Human Sciences, 1979.

Monahan, J., and Ruggiero, M. Psychological and psychiatric aspects of determinate criminal sentencing. *International Journal of Law and Psychiatry,* 1980, *3,* 105-116.

Monahan, J., and Splane, S. Psychological approaches to criminal behavior. In: Bittner, E., Messinger, S., eds. *Criminology Review Yearbook.* Beverly Hills, Calif.: Sage Publications, 1980.

Monahan, J., and Wexler, D. A definite maybe: Proofs and probability in civil commitment. *Law and Human Behavior,* 1978, *2,* 37-42.

Moos, R. Conceptualizations of human environments. *American Psychologist,* 1973, *28,* 652-665.

Moos, R. *Evaluating Correctional and Community Settings.* New York: Wiley, 1975.

Moos, R., and Insel, P. *Issues in Social Ecology.* Palo Alto, Calif.: National Press, 1973.

Morse, S. Crazy behavior, morals, and science: An analysis of the mental health legal system. *Southern California Law Review,* 1978, *51,* 527-654.

Mulvihill, D., and Tumin, M., eds. *Crimes of Violence: A Staff Report Submitted to the National Commission on the Causes and Prevention of Violence.* Washington, D.C.: Supt. of Docs., U.S. Print. Off., 1969.

Murphy, T. Michigan risk prediction: A replication study. Final Report, AP-). Lansing, Michigan: Department of Corrections Program Bureau, 1980.

National Council on Crime and Delinquency, Board of Directors. The nondangerous offender should not be imprisoned: A policy statement. *Crime and Delinquency*, 1973, *19*, 449-456.

National Institute of Mental Health. *Dangerous Behavior: A Problem in Law and Mental Health.* Frederick, C., ed. DHEW Pub. No. (ADM) 78-563. Washington, D.C.: Supt. of Docs., U.S. Govt. Print. Off., 1978, 37-60.

Newman, O. *Defensible Space.* New York: Macmillan, 1972.

Newton, G., and Zimring, F. *Firearms and Violence in American Life: Staff Report to the National Commission on the Causes and Prevention of Violence.* Washington, D.C.: Supt. of Docs., U.S. Govt. Print. Off., 1970.

Nisbett, R., Borgida, E., Crandall, R., and Reed, H. Popular induction: Information is not necessarily informative. In: Carroll, J., and Payne, J., eds. *Cognition and Social Behavior.* Hillsdale, N.J.: Erlbaum, 1976.

Novaco, R. *Anger Control: The Development and Evaluation of an Experimental Treatment.* Lexington, Mass.: Lexington Books, 1975.

Novaco, R. The function and regulation of the arousal of anger. *American Journal of Psychiatry*, 1976, *133*, 1124-1128.

Novaco, R. Anger and coping with stress. In: Foreyt, J., and Rathjen, D., eds. *Cognitive Behavior Therapy: Theory, Research and Practice.* New York: Plenum, 1978.

Novaco, R. The cognitive regulation of anger and stress. In: Kendall, P., and Hollon, S., eds. *Cognitive-Behavioral Interventions: Theory, Research, and Procedures.* New York: Academic Press, 1979, pp. 241-285.

Overholser v. *Russell* 282 Fed.2d 195, 1960.

Park, R. *The City.* Chicago: University of Chicago Press, 1925.

Peszke, M. Is dangerousness an issue for physicians in emergency commitment? *American Journal of Psychiatry*, 1975, *132*, 825-828.

Petersilia, J., Greenwood, P., and Lavin, M. *Criminal Careers of Habitual Felons.* Santa Monica, Calif.: Rand, 1977.

Pfohl, S. The psychiatric assessment of dangerousness: Practical problems and political implications. In: Conrad, J., and Dinitz, S., eds. *In Fear of Each Other.* Lexington, Mass: Lexington Books. 1977, pp. 77-101.

Pollock, H. Is the paroled patient a menace to the community? *Psychiatric Quarterly*, 1938, *12*, 236-244.

President's Commission on Mental Health. *Report to the President.* Washington, D.C.: Supt. of Docs., U.S. Govt. Print. Off., 1978.

Pritchard, D. Stable predictors of recidivism. *Journal Supplement Abstract Service*, 1977, *7*, 72.

PROMIS Research Project. *Highlights of Interim Findings and Implications.* Washington, D.C.: Institute for Law and Social Research, 1977.

Rabkin, J. Criminal behavior of discharged mental patients: A critical appraisal of the research. *Psychological Bulletin*, 1979, *86*, 1-27.

Rappaport, J. A response to "Implications from the Baxstrom experience." *Bulletin of the American Academy of Psychiatry and the Law*, 1973, *1*, 197-198.

Rappaport, J., and Lassen, G. Dangerousness-arrest rate comparisons of discharged patients and the general population. *American Journal of Psychiatry*, 1965, *121*, 776-783.

Rawls, J. *A Theory of Justice.* Cambridge, Mass.: Harvard University Press, 1972.

Rector, M. Who are the dangerous? *Bulletin of the American Academy of Psychiatry and the Law,* 1973, *1,* 186-188.

Rennie, Y. *The Search for Criminal Man: A Conceptual History of the Dangerous Offender.* Lexington, Mass.: Lexington Books, 1978.

Roth, L. Clinical and legal considerations in the therapy of violence-prone patients. In: Masserman, J., ed. *Current Psychiatric Therapies.* New York: Grune & Stratton, 1978, pp. 55-63.

Roth, L. A commitment law for patients, doctors, and lawyers. *American Journal of Psychiatry,* 1979, *136,* 1121-1127.

Roth, L., and Ervin, F. Psychiatric care of federal prisoners. *American Journal of Psychiatry,* 1971, *128,* 424-430.

Roth, L., and Meisel, A. Dangerousness, confidentiality and the duty to warn. *American Journal of Psychiatry,* 1977, *134,* 508-511.

Rubin, B. Prediction of dangerousness in mentally ill criminals. *Archives of General Psychiatry,* 1972, *72,* 397-407.

Rule, B., and Nesdale, A. Emotional arousal and aggressive behavior. *Psychological Bulletin,* 1976, *83,* 851-863.

Ryan, W. *Blaming the Victim.* New York: Random House, 1971.

Sarbin, T. The dangerous individual: An outcome of social identity transformations. *British Journal of Criminology,* July 1967, 285-295.

Sawyer, J. Measurement and prediction, clinical and statistical. *Psychological Bulletin,* 1966, *66,* 178-200.

Scharf, P. Inmate rights: A philosophic perspective. *Proceedings of the American Correctional Association,* in press.

Schmidt, P., and Witte, A. "Determinants of Criminal Recidivism: Further Investigations." Report to the North Carolina Department of Correction, 1978.

Scott, P. Assessing dangerousness in criminals. *British Journal of Psychiatry,* 1977, *131,* 127-142.

Shah, S. Dangerousness: Some definitional, conceptual and public policy issues. In: Sales, B., ed. *Perspectives in Law and Psychology.* New York: Plenum, 1977, pp. 91-119.

Shah, S. Dangerousness: A paradigm for exploring some issues in law and psychology. *American Psychologist,* 1978*a,* *33,* 224-238.

Shah, S. Dangerousness and mental illness. Some conceptual, prediction and policy dilemmas. In: Frederick, C., ed. *Dangerous Behavior: A Problem in Law and Mental Health.* NIMH. DHEW Publication No. (ADM) 78-563, Washington, D.C.: Supt. of Docs., Govt. Print. Off., 1978*b,* 153-191.

Shapiro, A. The evaluation of clinical prediction: A method and initial application. *New England Journal of Medicine, 296,* 1977, 1509-1514.

Shinnar, S., and Shinnar, R. The effects of the criminal justice system on the control of crime: A quantitative approach. *Law and Society Review,* 1975, *9,* 581-611.

Silberman, C. *Criminal Violence, Criminal Justice.* New York: Random House, 1978.

Skodol, A., and Karasu, T. Emergency psychiatry and the assaultive patient. *American Journal of Psychiatry,* 1978, *135,* 202-205.

Sosowsky, L. Crime and violence among mental patients reconsidered in view of the new legal relationship between the state and the mentally ill. *American Journal of Psychiatry,* 1978, *135,* 33-42.

State of Maryland. "Maryland's Defective Delinquency Statute–A Progress Report." Unpublished manuscript. Department of Public Safety and Correctional Services, 1978.

State of Michigan. "Summary of Parolee Risk Study." Unpublished manuscript, Department of Corrections, 1978.

Steadman, H. The psychiatrist as a conservative agent of social control. *Social Problems,* 1972, *20,* 263-271.

Steadman, H. A new look at recidivism among Patuxent inmates. *The Bulletin of the American Academy of Psychiatry and the Law,* 1977, *5,* 200-209.

Steadman, H., and Cocozza, J. *Careers of the Criminally Insane.* Lexington, Mass.: Lexington Books, 1974.

Steadman, H., and Cocozza, J. Selective reporting and the public misconceptions of the criminally insane. *Public Opinion Quarterly,* 1978, *4,* 523-533.

Steadman, H., Cocozza, J., and Melick, M. Explaining the increased crime rate of mental patients: The changing clientele of State hospitals. *American Journal of Psychiatry,* 1978, *135,* 816-820.

Steadman, H., and Halton, A. The Baxstrom patients: Backgrounds and outcome. *Seminars in Psychiatry,* 1971, *3,* 376-386.

Steadman, H., and Keveles, C. The community adjustment and criminal activity of the Baxstrom patients: 1966-1960. *American Journal of Psychiatry,* 1972, *129,* 304-310.

Steadman, H., Vanderwyst, D., and Ribner, S. Comparing arrest rates of mental patients and criminal offenders. *American Journal of Psychiatry,* 1978, *135,* 1218-1220.

Stokols, D., ed. *Psychological Perspectives on Environment and Behavior: Conceptual and Empirical Trends.* New York: Plenum Press, 1977.

Stone, A. *Mental Health and the Law: A System in Transition.* NIMH. DHEW Publication No. (ADM) 76-176. Washington, D.C.: Supt. of Docs., U.S. Govt. Print. Off., 1975.

Sweetland, J. " 'Illusory Correlation' and the Estimation of 'Dangerous' Behavior." Unpublished dissertation, Department of Psychology, Indiana University, 1972.

Szasz, T. *Law, Liberty and Psychiatry.* New York: Macmillan, 1963.

Tarasoff v. *Regents of the University of California,* Sup. 131 Cal. Rptr, 14, 1976.

Terkel, S. *Working.* New York: Pantheon, 1974.

Thornberry, T., and Jacoby, J. "The Uses of Discretion in a Maximum Security Mental Hospital: The Dixon Case." Presented at the annual meeting of the American Society of Criminology, Chicago, 1974.

Thornberry, T., and Jacoby, J. *The Criminally Insane: A Community Follow-up of Mentally Ill Offenders.* Chicago: University of Chicago Press, 1979.

Tittle, C.; Villemez, W.; and Smith, D. The myth of social class and criminality: An empirical assessment of the empirical evidence. *American Sociological Review,* 1978, *43,* 643-656.

Toch, H. *Violent Men.* Chicago: Aldine, 1969.

Tversky, A., and Kahneman, D. Judgment under uncertainty: Heuristics and biases. *Science,* 1974, *185,* 1124-1131.

Tversky, A., and Kahneman, D. Causal schemata in judgments under uncertainty. In: Fishbein, M., ed. *Progress in Social Psychology.* Hillsdale, N.J.: Erlbaum, in press.

Twentieth Century Fund. *Fair and Certain Punishment.* New York: McGraw-Hill, 1976.

Underwood, B. Law and the crystal ball: Predicting behavior with statistical inference and individualized judgment. *Yale Law Journal,* 1979, *88,* 1408-1448.

von Hirsch, A. *Doing Justice: The Choice of Punishments.* New York: Hill & Wang, 1976.

Webster, W. *Crime in the United States–1977.* F.B.I. Washington, D.C.: Supt. of Docs., U.S. Govt. Print. Off., 1978.

Weinberg, A., ed. *Attorney for the Damned.* New York: Simon & Schuster, 1957.

Wenk, E., Robison, J., and Smith, G. Can violence be predicted? *Crime and Delinquency,* 1972, *18,* 393-402.

Wexler, D. Patients, therapists, and third parties: The victimoligical virtues of *Tarasoff. International Journal of Law and Psychiatry,* 1979, *2,* 1-28.

Wicker, A. Processes which mediate behavior-environment congruence. *Behavioral Science,* 1972, *17,* 265-277.

Wilkins, L., Kress, J., Gottfredson, D., Calpin, J., and Gelman, A. *Sentencing guidelines and structuring judicial discretion.* L.E.A.A. Washington, D.C.: Supt. of Docs., U.S. Govt. Print. Off., 1978.

Williams, W., and Miller, K. The role of personal characteristics in perceptions of dangerousness. *Criminal Justice and Behavior,* 1977, *4,* 421.

Wilson, J. The political feasibility of punishment. In: Cederblom, J., and Blizek, W., eds. *Justice and Punishment,* Cambridge, Mass.: Ballinger, 1977, pp. 107-123.

Wise, T. Where the public peril begins: A survey of psychotherapists to determine the effects of Tarasoff. *Stanford Law Review,* 1978, *31,* 165-190.

Wolfgang, M. *Patterns in Criminal Homicide.* Philadelphia: University of Pennsylvania Press, 1958.

Wolfgang, M. "From Boy to Man–From Delinquency to Crime." National Symposium on the Serious Juvenile Offender, Minneapolis, 1977.

Wolfgang, M. "An Overview of Research into Violent Behavior." Testimony before the U.S. House of Representatives Committee on Science and Technology, 1978.

Wolfgang, M., Figlio, R., and Sellin, T. *Delinquency in a Birth Cohort.* Chicago: University of Chicago Press, 1972.

Zimring, F. Determinants of the death rate from robbery: A Detroit time study. *Journal of Legal Studies,* 1977, VI, 317-332.

Zimring, F. Background paper. In: *Confronting Youth Crime: Report of the Twentieth Century Fund Task Force in Sentencing Policy Toward Young Offenders.* New York: Holmes and Meier, 1978, pp. 27-120.

Zitrin, A., Hardesty, A., Burdock, E., and Drosaman, J. Crime and violence among mental patients. *American Journal of Psychiatry,* 1976, *133,* 142-149.

ABOUT THE AUTHOR

John Monahan is a psychologist and Professor of Law in the School of Law, Psychiatry and Public Policy, University of Virginia. He was previously at the Program in Social Ecology and the Department of Psychiatry at the University of California, Irvine, and has been a Fellow in Law and Psychology at Harvard Law School and Stanford Law School. He chaired the American Psychological Association's Task Force on the Role of Psychology in the Criminal Justice System, was a member of the Panel on Legal Issues of the President's Commission on Mental Health and of the Panel of Offender Rehabilitation of the National Academy of Sciences, and is a past-president of the American Psychology-Law Society. Monahan has testified before congressional and state legislative committees on matters of mental health and criminal justice policy, and his work in this area has been cited in decisions of the U.S. Supreme Court, the California Supreme Court, and other judicial bodies.